Prisoners in D
A Skippy Dare M

Percy Keese Fitzhugh

Alpha Editions

This edition published in 2024

ISBN 9789362517388

Design and Setting By
Alpha Editions
www.alphaedis.com
Email - info@alphaedis.com

Contents

CHAPTER I

ON THE TRAIL

When Skippy Dare entered the big office building he found himself in an enchanted realm. He had never before visited one of these commercial palaces and he gazed about him in speechless awe. He found the revolving door so delightful that it seemed like some freakish entertainment in an amusement park, and he indulged himself with the giddy sensation of going around and around in it until a uniformed elevator starter brusquely ordered him out.

Instead, he went in.

Observing the rather ornate cigar and candy booth, he invested in a gooey chocolate bar which he ate while studying the alphabetical list of offices. He was deeply impressed with this imposing directory and experienced a thrill of triumph when at last his searching eyes discovered the name, INTERNATIONAL DETECTIVE AGENCY—7-721-728.

He was now on the trail, he told himself, though, to be sure, the least false move might prove fatal (a phrase which he had read in a detective story) for the eye of the starter was still upon him and he did not look the more kindly on Skippy because of the liquefied chocolate which now decorated the border of the boy's mouth. His spirit mounted when he had attained the safety of a gorgeous elevator where every thrill of its dizzy ascent brought him nearer to the famous detective agency's offices.

Skippy, you must know, longed to be a great sleuth. He had lately read in a newspaper of the rounding up of a gang of counterfeiters by the famous Carlton Conne, head of the International office. That was the spark which brought about the certainty that apprehending criminals was the career which a kindly fate would offer him.

It must be understood that there was some color of reason to this bizarre choice of a vocation. He had grown up on the waterfront among characters sufficiently dubious. Few detectives, however great their prowess and renown, had come into so much personal contact with the lawless element of the river front as had Skippy. A motherless urchin since infancy and lacking paternal care for a period in which his father had been unjustly jailed, his forced association with this motley crew had given him a remarkable insight about people in general.

That Skippy's father was at last liberated and his good name restored is not a part of this narrative. Suffice it to say, that the hapless man did not long survive after his liberation. He left his young and lonely son to the tender mercies of an aunt who lived on the east side of the great city. And, though Skippy was destined to have many narrow escapes in the course of his spectacular career, perhaps the narrowest of all was his escape from being put in an orphan asylum.

Like many great men he was denied the benefit of an early education. Mrs. Kinney, weak in finances but strong in resolve, triumphed over the Board of Education, and Skippy was given working papers which conferred on him the inestimable privilege of earning his living.

So we find him stepping out of the elevator on the seventh floor of the mammoth office building whistling blithely, yet distinctly conscious of the long trousers (his first) which were such an integral part of the new six dollar suit he was wearing. His aunt had parted with this enormous sum only because of the inauguration of his business career.

On the door of room 721 was the magic word ENTER and Skippy paused with his hand on the knob, giving himself a delicious moment before making the grand plunge. It may be that he fully expected to see a handcuffed burglar or two when he opened the door. But no such thrilling sight awaited him. There was nothing more startling than a richly furnished waiting room at the end of which sat a pretty young lady.

She peered over her gleaming mahogany typewriter desk and paused in her typing with an air of bored expectancy.

"Well?"

"I gotta—eh, I wanta ... see ... Mr. Carlton Conne," Skippy stammered.

She extended her hand as if by force of habit and said wearily, "You have a letter to deliver?"

"Nope. I—I wanta see Mr. Conne."

"Oh, you can't see Mr. Conne. He's a very busy man. What do you want?"

"I wanta job."

"We don't need any boys now." The young lady yawned discreetly. "If you want to leave your name and address we'll send for you if an opening occurs. Did someone send you here?" she asked, handing him a slip of paper and a pencil.

"Nope. I bin wantin' to work for Mr. Conne since I first read about him in the papers. I wanta learn from him how to be a regular detective like him. That's the kinda job I want."

At this naïve confession the girl laughed while Skippy, embarrassed, but still persistent, stood waiting. "So lemme see him?" he urged.

"No, certainly not," the girl answered a little tersely. "I told you that Mr. Conne is a very busy man and he's a very important man—if you know what that means. He doesn't see boys. If we should need an office boy, we can send for you," she added with an air of finality.

It was a crucial moment to Skippy. He gave a furtive look toward a closed door, beyond which, in some holy of holies, he imagined the great Carlton Conne to be seated. He visualized that shrewd mouth and those keen eyes which he had seen pictured in the newspapers at the astonishing climax of the famous Hawley murder case. But there was no hope. Skippy Dare was baffled by a mere girl at the very threshold of the lion's den.

Suddenly the door opened and a trim looking young man emerged. It was not the great Carlton Conne. Very casually, it seemed, he closed the door and leaned against it.

"He one of 'em?" he asked briskly.

"Oh, no," said the girl.

"Well, I wish you'd get in touch up there with the principal, or one of the teachers or somebody, and see if they can't round up two or three of the kids who were run down. They ought to be able to identify one or two of the gang in that stolen car. According to the wop that keeps the banana stand, there were a bunch of 'em coming out of school when the car ploughed through. There must be at least two who could make some identification. The chief wants to get at least two of 'em down as soon as possible."

"I'll see what I can do, but if the two who were run down were the only ones that could identify...."

"Well, you know the chief; he wants what he wants when he wants it. Even if their necks were broken he'd expect 'em to remember whether or not they saw a machine gun in that car. So that's that."

The girl seemed listlessly tolerant. "I'll get in touch with them as soon as I come back from lunch. Will that do?"

The young man nodded and the door closed behind him. Skippy too departed, thoughtfully, hopefully, and with machine guns booming in his active brain. *Gangsters, a stolen car!* The International was on the trail of something.

The question uppermost in his mind was—how long a time would the typist remain out at lunch? He hurried down the hall, then darted into the shadow of a stairway from which vantage point he could keep his bright eyes on the International Agency's door.

There was no doubt of it now—Skippy too was on the trail of something.

CHAPTER II

CRASHING IN

It was only a matter of seconds when the door of the International offices opened and the pretty typist stepped into the hall. Her high heels clicked briskly along the tiled floor and she looked neither to the right nor left, but hurried straight to the elevators.

Skippy, meanwhile, had backed down farther into the shadow and was standing on the landing, his slim body almost rigid against the cool wall. There was a moment's silence in which he stood tense, listening, until at last the metallic clang of the elevator door opening and closing echoed down to him.

He relaxed immediately and his face crinkled in a smile. With a weather eye on the landing above and the landing below he hastily removed his coat and tore from his new white shirt a goodly strip of the muslin. This had the effect of setting his collar and tie somewhat awry but he hadn't time to worry over that detail. He was too busy improvising a presentable sling in which to rest his left arm. He had a momentary impulse to bandage his head also, but he was too true an artist to overdo the thing.

Be that as it may, luck was with him, for a moment later, when he presented himself at the International offices, he found a small group of men, presumably detectives, talking earnestly in the reception room. One glance at Skippy and two of the men hurried forward to open the door just beyond.

"Here y'are, kid—this way," said one, smilingly. "You'll see a door to your right marked *Carlton Conne—Private*—that's where you're to go. Mr. Conne wants to see some of you kids."

Skippy grinned amiably.

He was not afraid, as he trudged manfully into the holy of holies to confront the famous head of the world-renowned detective agency, whose picture he had so many times seen in the newspapers.

The great detective was not an awe-inspiring spectacle. He sat in his shirt sleeves, his chair tilted back and his feet resting on the desk. He was a stocky, middle-aged man with a bristly moustache and a crisp, aggressive look. Also he was smoking a long black cigar (Skippy soon learned that this was a fixed habit with the man) which he dexterously moved from one end of his mouth to the other as he talked. When he listened, he had a way of tilting it at an upright angle which gave him a very shrewd and sophisticated air. It was this attitude that captivated Skippy.

"Well," he said in his gruff, yet kindly manner, "you're one of the kids that got in the way of that stolen car, eh? Your arm's busted, eh?"

"No sir," Skippy answered promptly with unabashed frankness. "My name's Skippy Dare an' I just wanted to get in here—kind of—so—so I could talk to you. But...."

Carlton Conne brought his feet down from the desk and stared. "But the sling—what's it for?"

"That typewriter girl," said Skippy rapidly, "she said I couldn't see you about a job—that you didn't need nobody."

"You mean you talked to Miss Purdy, our reception clerk?" asked the detective with an enigmatic scowl.

"Yeah, I guess that's who it was. She was in that first room out there with the big soft rug an' she was pretty all right, but she was cranky an' wouldn't lissen. I tried to tell her I wanted a job right away an' be a detective an'...."

Carlton Conne lifted his feet from the floor and set them back again on the desk. He shifted the cigar about in his mouth three or four times, then interposed: "So you got in here under false pretenses, eh?" Before Skippy could answer, he added, "What put the sling idea into your head?"

"While I was talkin' to the—to Miss Purdy, a feller come out an' said about the stolen car an' all an' how you wanted the kids that was run down so's you could talk to 'em. So right away I thought about the sling an' I sneaked into the hall an' hid on the stairway till she goes out for lunch. Then I fixed the sling from the taila my shirt.... I'll be good at disguises, Mr. Conne—that's why I know I'd be a good detective."

"Oh, you do, eh?" A mirthful gleam lighted the detective's eyes, but his face was wrinkled into a scowl. "I suppose your other disguise today consists of working papers, eh? You can't be more than fourteen."

"Gee, how'd you guess!"

Carlton Conne looked at the boy sharply. "S'pose you've been blowing in all your spending money on cheap detective magazines and going to these rotten mystery thrillers, eh?"

"Nope, I don't like them magazines, Mr. Conne. An' I don't like mystery thrillers 'cause I ain't so dumb that I don't know those things couldn't happen in real life. Gee, I can only go to the movies once in a while an' when I go I like to see somepin' that makes me laugh. Since my father died I don't get no spendin' money 'cause my aunt's terrible poor an' she says I gotta be glad she can even lemme sleep an' eat."

"And she had to put you out to work?" Carlton Conne tilted his cigar thoughtfully. "And you decided you wanted to be a detective. Why?"

"I always wanted to be a detective," Skippy answered unabashed, "ever since they railroaded my father. When they let him out I wanted to be one more'n ever an' when he died an' I come back to lookin' for my aunt I almost was sent to Reform 'cause I got hungry an' went into a restaurant an' ate a whole lot more'n I had the money to pay for. So anyway they found my aunt an' she took me from the station house an' promised to take care of me. But all the time since, I been thinkin' how if I was a detective I'd know the difference between a kid that was bad and a kid that was hungry. Gee, I know crooks like anything, Mr. Conne, so that's another reason I'd make a good detective. A bunch of 'em lived 'round me when I was on the barge waitin' for my father to get outa jail. River pirates an' all! They're my special—my specialty!" he bragged.

"And 'Reform's' your special fear, eh?" Carlton Conne asked, blinking his eyes.

"Yeah, I was scareda that like anythin'," Skippy admitted with a shudder at the memory. "When my father was on trial I shivered in my boots afraid they'd send me there."

Carlton Conne brought his feet down onto the softly carpeted floor and pulling up his chair, scrutinized a letter that lay open on his desk. After a moment's silence he glanced up at the boy and swiftly surveyed him.

"Suppose I were to tell you that I want you to go to Reform School!" he said enigmatically.

"Huh?" Skippy asked, wide-eyed.

"Sit down!" Carlton Conne said briskly. "I want to talk to you!"

Skippy did as he was told.

CHAPTER III

A BARGAIN

Carlton Conne took the letter in his hand and manoeuvered the cigar back and forth in his mouth. At length he said, "Don't be scared, kid. I want you to go, but not for anything *you've* done—it's for me!"

Skippy gasped. "Gee, you mean you're gonna lemme be a detec——"

"Listen, kid," the man interposed kindly, "get that detective idea out of your head until you're—well say, twenty-four years old anyhow. You have to learn, kid, and it takes long, hard years—it's just another kind of school. But right now I can use a kid like you—you can be of some use to me. If you do your work right—keep your eyes open, your mouth shut and remember everything, I might consider you for the job as office boy at fifteen dollars a week. In the mean time, I'm to have you sent to the Delafield Reformatory where you're going to play the part you almost had in real life—a boy unjustly sent there and a boy who'd make a break for freedom at the first opportunity."

"Then—then you ain't gonna send me for real!" Skippy stammered joyfully. "I'm just sorta gonna play de—*detective?*"

"You're going to help *me!*" answered Conne with the hint of a smile on his face. "You're going to play the part of a reform school kid as I told you before. And I'm counting on you to play it with the same kind of energy that made you sling up your arm so that you could get in here to see me. That's why I'm going to trust you to do this thing for me! You've got ingenuity—know what that means, kid?"

"Yeah," Skippy smiled, "it means havin' swell ideas that go through."

"In a measure, yes. Anyway, you've the idea and you have ingenuity, whether or not you know what it means. But the question is, can I count on you not to let anyone know (except those whom I authorize to keep in touch with you) who you are, nor the part you're playing? You may have to play it a month, perhaps longer—I can't tell you how long, kid. Think you could play it without betraying your game by a look or a word?"

"Gee, Mr. Conne—gee, is it sorta dangerous like? I mean I can do that about keepin' my mouth shut an' all—I learned that when my father got in trouble—nobody could make me tell a thing. I mean will it be dangerous if I *did* tell? Not that I would—honest, Mr. Conne!"

"That's what I thought, kid. I wouldn't have asked you otherwise. And as for its being dangerous," said Mr. Conne tipping his cigar so that the lighted end stood dangerously near his nose, "I wouldn't allow you to do it if it was. Of course there's bound to be a minimum of danger in anything of this kind, but we'll prepare you for that. If you stick and keep your mouth shut there's nothing to be feared. One of my men will be on hand as soon as the conditions warrant it. If your aunt consents, I'll assume full responsibility for you."

"Aw, my aunt don't care so long's I ain't no expense to her. I gotta terrible appetite, Mr. Conne, an' she says I eat her out of house an' home an' besides she wants back the six dollars she paid out for my suit. She wants it to pay on insurance, she says."

"Very well, kid—she'll have it. After I get through telling you a little more of this job, you can go home and get her and bring her down here to me. I'll talk to her and if she's agreeable, I'll give her your first week's salary. She knows your needs better than you do, I guess."

"Yeah," said Skippy amiably. "Aunt Min'll save for me, she says, so's I'll have some money in bank when I grow up. She said if I got a job she'd give me money for carfare an' for a little spendin' money."

"She can do that after you've done this work and are working regularly in this office. Just now, while you're temporary, I'll pay you your expenses and give your aunt your salary. How's that?"

"Sure, whatever you say, Mr. Conne," Skippy answered happily. "You pay me more when it's sorta extra work, huh?"

"That's the basis on which all our men work here, kid," the detective grinned. "When your time is on the company, naturally your expenses are too. But leave that to me—I'll see that you have enough to eat in the way of chocolate even if you do leave half of it on your chin."

Skippy grinned and reached for his handkerchief. When he had rubbed off the smear, he looked up. "Will you tell me some more about this job?"

Carlton Conne nodded and smoothed out the letter on his desk. "This is a report from one of my men who was on a case in Chicago," he was saying. "To let you know more fully about this job I'll read part of this report: 'Ran across O'Reilly here in Chi,' he says, 'and he tells me that Dean Devlin is suspected of helping to spring a kid by the name of Tucker from the South End Reform School here. They picked the kid up in Wheaton and when brought back to Chi he told, under pressure, that a reverend-looking gentleman whose description fits the Dean to a "T" visited the South End Reform a little more than a month ago and propositioned him. The kid was bent to beat it and the Dean gave him some dough for a getaway.

"'Anyway, out of this money, Tucker was told to bribe a guard and the Dean arranged the night of the escape, etc. Tucker said it was soft—the Dean was on the job in a closed car and took him to a house in what looked to be a nice part of the city. It was a pretty swell flat and the kid got everything he wanted in the way of eats, but he was kept a prisoner along with two other kids his own age who, it seemed, were also under the Dean's protection. They too had crashed out of different reform schools under the reverend-looking gentleman's expert supervision.

"'Now it seems that Devlin's idea was this: each kid was kept on at the flat till he found a job for them in some distant city. Then he saw to it that the kid got there. And so within a month, Tucker saw the other kids go. Then Devlin told Tucker that he had a job for him out in Montana, and that very night he was going to drive him as far as Alton where he could board a train absolutely safe from suspicion.

"'They started after dark and Tucker said it wasn't long before he got drowsy. He thinks he must have fallen asleep for the next thing he knew he felt himself falling against something and then he seemed to fall right out of the car and whirl through the air. Next thing he knew he was in the water. The car had gone down and he knew that he'd go down too, not being able to swim. He paddled furiously with his hands and looking up on the bank he saw the Dean standing there looking down. Tucker was just about to call to him when a car drove up and Devlin got in it and was driven away.

"'Evidently, the Dean was afraid that Tucker hadn't survived the accident and being himself confessedly nervous of the police (that being the reason for his generous interest in reform school boys) he thought it best to get away as quickly as possible by hailing the first car that came along.'"

"Gee, an' what did poor Tucker do then, huh?" Skippy asked excitedly.

Carlton Conne smiled. "Fortunately for him, he had been thrown clear of the car and into shallow water. Just when he had resigned himself to a watery grave, he thrust his legs out and found that his feet touched bottom. You can bet that he didn't lose any time in scrambling up the high embankment to safety."

"An' did he let that Devlin know that, huh?"

Carlton Conne studied the letter before him and shook his round head. "No, he couldn't. You see he had only seen the street and the house itself at night. After all, he had been imprisoned for a month and both the street and the house looked just like a hundred others in Chicago. Devlin had driven him to and from the house in such a hurry that he never had the chance to see where he had been living. He decided to get as far away from

Chicago and the police as he could. But he was picked up in a place called Wheaton, anyway."

"Boy, what luck!" was Skippy's sympathetic exclamation.

"Seeing it from your point of view—yes. From my point of view, it's fortunate that Tucker lost out, for it has warmed up a trail that's been cold too long. Devlin has been under cover a couple of years now. O'Reilly, who is an inspector on the Chicago force, said they're anxious to find out where the other two kids are that the Dean helped to crash out of reform schools. Well, Dick Hallam knows that I'll be interested to know why, for I got some old scores to settle with the Dean and like a good detective he got the Dean's scent and has trailed him to New York. This morning he learned that our reverend-looking friend has applied for a permit to visit the Delafield Reform School next Friday. That's the reason, kid, that I want you to be there when he shows up."

"Hot dog, Mr. Conne! I been dumb not to see what you meant before. Gee whiz, you want me there to trap him like, huh?"

"I want you to be there to help me to prepare the trap, kid. None of my men can palm themselves off as kids and it seems that Devlin has been playing up to kids only. That's why you're going to Delafield. You're going to help me find out why he's been acting so generous when I know that he isn't the type of man to do anything like that without there being money in it somewhere. Dean Devlin never did anything for nothing. And so you're going to put yourself in his way when he makes that visit on Friday—I'll see to it that you have every opportunity. What's more, you're going to fall in with any plans he may make for you."

"Boy, it sounds terrible excitin', Mr. Conne!"

"Not dangerously so," the detective assured him. "One of our men, Dorcas is his name, will either go up with you or be up there on Friday and so be on hand if you need him. You'll have no cause to worry—you won't be alone at any time if you do just as you're told. But there won't be any real danger, kid—I wouldn't let you into this if there was. Dean Devlin is a notorious swindler and blackmailer and though he can cause plenty of excitement when he's on the trail, I've never heard of him laying a hand on anybody. He's after money, not people."

"Gee whiz," Skippy said stoutly, "I wouldn't be afraid anyhow!"

"That's why I've taken an interest in you, kid. All you want is nerve—courage enough to go through with your part, and keep your mind and eyes on all that Dean Devlin does and says. You've got a job and I might as well warn you that how well you do it will determine your permanent employment by this company. In other words, it's to be your entrance exam, so you better try to pass it!"

"Gee, will I pass it!" Skippy cried exultantly. "You'll see how I'm gonna pass it, Mr. Conne!"

"That's the talk, kid," the detective said with a half-smile. "And when Dean Devlin is where he can't take any more money from my clients or anybody else, I'll talk to you about staying on for a regular job."

CHAPTER IV

JOHN DOE

In the Juvenile Court next day, Skippy was duly arraigned and sentenced. An International Detective Agency man posing as an irate merchant pressed a charge of petty larceny against John Doe, orphan, no home and a native of the city of New York. The evening papers carried a small first page story on this original John Doe who was about to spend his first night of a four year sentence in the Delafield Reformatory.

Meanwhile, Skippy was aware that his role of John Doe, thief, had become almost too realistic to be comfortable. His morning wait in the courtroom had seemed interminable. The heat was oppressive, the court procedure tiresome and he felt not a little regret that he had not urged Mr. Conne to have his aunt come and give him the bit of encouragement he needed to go on with his part in the reformatory. He thought of his dead father, of Big Joe Tully who had lost his life saving the Airedale, Mugs, which he had given to Skippy. And Mugs too was gone, killed by an auto.

Not that he felt in the least fearful nor doubted his ability to go through with his strange role. He merely felt a little lonesome and wished that he might look out over the sea of faces that crowded the courtroom and see his Aunt Min's among them, smiling her encouragement. But his aunt was at home busy with her sewing that morning, quite content with the money that Carlton Conne had turned over to her and satisfied that the great detective would see that her nephew was safe and sound.

Skippy had to be content with the presence of Dick Hallam, Carlton Conne's man, notwithstanding the fact that he was supposed to be prosecuting him. Hallam, however, was better than no one at all for when the occasion permitted, he flashed a significant look at the boy.

He spent the afternoon in an ante room and Dick Hallam, blond, tall and about twenty-eight, played "rummy" with him. Also, he had too much to eat, including ice cream and candy and cold drinks and at about four o'clock Carlton Conne came in.

"All set, kid?" he asked with that half-smile that Skippy was beginning to like.

"*And how!*" the boy grinned, feeling cheerful immediately.

"He's been acting like it's a picnic, boss," Dick Hallam interposed gaily.

"Fine," said the detective. "You want to keep it up, kid—you've nothing to fear—not a thing! Everything's been arranged, and I don't think you'll have to spend more than a night or two at Delafield. Meanwhile, what time you *do* spend, you'll have someone watching close at hand so never feel you're alone. The warden and a few trusted guards know of our little game, but of course you're to speak to no one about it unless you're spoken to first. Now—you remember all the signals?"

"Yes sir—everythin'!"

Dick Hallam grinned. "He's just nervous about riding up with that rough neck gang that's been sentenced today, boss. Especially one tough kid named Nickie Fallon who got seven years for trying his hand at a hold-up and carrying a gun. Some character, that kid."

"I know," Conne said understandingly, "that's the only disagreeable part of this job, kid. But I warned you what the company would be like."

"Aw gee, Mr. Conne, I ain't afraida that. I was just wonderin' if they'd be the kind of guys what start a fight on the way an' if they did what would I do, huh?"

"How would you act if you were riding up with that bunch to start a real sentence, eh? Well kid, get yourself in the state of mind that it is real and act accordingly."

Skippy did just that. About six o'clock a court attendant led him out to a closed car. Four boys ranging from about his own age to seventeen years sat inside and eyed him sullenly as he crowded his slim body among them to make the fifth passenger on the back seat. Two detectives followed and took the chairs before them; another detective sat ahead on the seat beside the driver.

"Well, if it ain't John Doe—the kid hisself!" a hoarse voice whispered beside him.

Skippy looked up and saw a drooping mouth and black eyes almost too bright—Nickie Fallon. Despite an inward shudder, he nodded and smiled.

"That's me," he said simply. "Got enough room?"

"Nah, but that's all jake. Might's well get used to crowdin'." Then, after a pause: "Say, you John Doe, on the level?"

Skippy gave a sidelong glance at the detectives to see if they noted this whispered conversation between Nickie Fallon and himself. Apparently they didn't, and he gave the boy another smile.

"Anyways, they slipped you four years, eh? Three years less'n me." There was another pause after which Fallon whispered, "They ain't keepin' me two days if I can take it on the lam. How about you, kid?"

Skippy nodded again, feeling rather foolish as he did so. However, he could think of no other course to pursue, and instinct prompted him to hold his tongue until he was sure of himself.

"Ain't the gabby kind, eh?" said the other. "Well, that's the kinda pal I like. Say, if they don't put us near each other up there, I'll raise the dust— see? I wanta pal like you."

Skippy stirred uneasily. Was Nickie Fallon going to be an unlooked-for factor in this strange play?

CHAPTER V

A FRIENDLY FACE

The Delafield Reform School was situated not far from the New Jersey state line. Therefore, the route over which the boys were taken was through a part of northeastern New Jersey, first crossing the great bridge which bears the magic name of George Washington.

It was upon entering the vast span that Nickie Fallon made known to Skippy his resolve. After that he lapsed into a long silence, looking past his new-found pal and out upon the gleaming concrete lanes that flanked them on both sides. His too-bright eyes seemed to roam through space and for a moment his gaze rested on the giant cables that stretched between sky and water like monstrous birds poised for flight.

Skippy had no doubt but that Nickie's thoughts were also on flight. The detectives, however, seemed not to be cognizant of it, for they were laughing and talking in low tones and apparently easy in mind about the safety of their charges.

Dusk was settling and the broad plaza on the New Jersey side of the bridge was resplendent with the last rays of the setting sun. Very swiftly they left it behind and whisked down under a broad concrete arch which brought them to a highway practically devoid of traffic.

"Ain't many people travelin' our way," a boy commented on the farther side of the seat. He was no more than sixteen, red-haired and with small blue eyes.

"Dippy Donovan's his name," Fallon informed Skippy immediately. "He drew a year for wreckin' the principal's office in school. Twict he done the same thing so now he's got his bit. I don't see doin' a stretch for anything like that. At least I got some dough outa what *I* done—how about *you*?"

"Yeah," Skippy murmured. And in order to divert the conversation from himself, he asked, "Who's the kid next you an' who's the one 'long-side him?"

"Greek pickpockets—Shorty an' Biff; don't ast me their last names! I can't pronounce 'em."

Skippy grinned and turned his head away looking off into the dusk. He was thinking that everything had gone fine so far and his behavior must certainly have impressed Nickie, for that youthful transgressor seemed to have accepted him at face value as one of his own kind.

It was during these reflections that Skippy noticed the detective sitting up in the seat beside the driver. He was a thin, lanky sort of man with hollow eyes and just at that moment he was glancing at the boys. Presently his gaze rested on Skippy and without warning he pursed his lips significantly and a look flashed from his eyes that the boy immediately understood.

One of Mr. Conne's men!

He turned his head away again so quickly that, under other circumstances, Skippy might have been inclined to consider the look as merely a figment of his imagination. But in this instance, he knew that he was right and that the detective had deliberately caught his attention to assure him of his helpful presence there as Mr. Conne's representative.

Well, it was helpful certainly, and tremendously reassuring to Skippy. Mr. Conne had kept his word so far and the play gave great promise of a successful conclusion. The boy was happier now and no longer felt alone in his new venture. He had a staunch and dependable supporter and all was well!

The shadows were lengthening and a lone bird winging swiftly homeward for the night, looked dark and small against the feeble light on the distant horizon. Talk lagged, then ceased altogether, and when night enfolded them in one vast black shadow no sound could be heard save the monotonous hum of the engine and the soft swish of the tires upon the concrete road.

After a little while they turned off into a dirt road. The powerful headlights gleamed out over deep ruts and in places the sandy soil lay in little mounds, causing the car to bump and flounder about from one side of the road to the other.

"Can't slow down too much," the driver said to the detectives. "I'm due back at ten and it's after eight now."

"It's O. K. with us," said one of the men sitting in back. He nodded at the man beside the driver. "You're not afraid of being thrown out either, are you, Dorcas?"

"If I am I can pick myself up again," came the reply. The speaker turned and though it was too dark to see very clearly, Skippy thought the man smiled at him.

So Dorcas was his name!

Glad of that additional knowledge, Skippy put from him any lingering fears. He was confident that nothing would mar Mr. Conne's well laid plans. Dorcas would always be there at Delafield.

They were still bumping along at a pretty fair speed when the engine emitted peculiar sounds. The driver made some comment but did not stop, saying that it was probably due to the gas which he was trying for the first time.

The engine continued to "act up" as the driver called it, but he did not lessen his speed. They seemed to bump in and out of the ruts faster than ever. Suddenly the car lurched forward tumbling them all about. And, while Skippy strove frantically to keep himself from falling entirely off the seat, they lurched again.

The driver yelled, the brakes ground and for the fraction of a second the powerful car seemed to whirl. Skippy felt himself whirled along with it, his head struck something and amid the ear-splitting shouts and screams from the boys and the men, there came the sound of breaking glass.

There was a sickening crash after that, but Skippy did not hear it.

CHAPTER VI

A SUSPICION

Skippy's head throbbed painfully and there was a soreness all over his slim body when he tried to move. His ears buzzed and his eyes opened with difficulty upon a world that was dark and confusing. Voices, low and hoarse, seemed all about him and he had the sensation of rapid motion that added materially to his discomfort.

It came to him gradually that he was neither lying down nor standing up, but that he was in a half-reclining position with his head resting on someone's lap. Also, he discovered that he was again in a car and that they seemed to be speeding along in the dark the same as before.

His head was being jounced up and down sending sharp pains through his body, and when he felt he could no longer stand it, he stirred. A familiar, hoarse voice spoke directly above him.

"Feelin' kinda rocky, pal?"

Skippy squinted but it was too dark to discern anything. Nevertheless, he sensed Nickie Fallon's bright eyes looking down at him inquiringly.

"You, Fallon?" he asked weakly.

"Yeah. Your head's been banged up an' I been holdin' you on my lap." Then, reassuringly: "But you'll be O. K., kid—don't worry."

"It's dark—terrible dark...."

"Yeah, we're travelin' without no lights. I'd keep kinda quiet if I was you. It ain't gonna be long 'fore we'll be where you can tumble in bed an' sleep till your head's better."

"He'll have nice eat—eh?" came a query in a slightly foreign accent. "Us will too, eh?"

A man's deep, sonorous voice from up in front answered in the affirmative. Nickie Fallon bent closer to Skippy's buzzing ears and explained, "That guy's name's Barker an' the one drivin's his pal, Frost. They're our pals from now on. Say, what a break they gave us!"

Skippy was deeply puzzled. He couldn't seem to make it out at all. "Those Greeks," he asked wearily, "didn't I hear one of 'em just now?"

"Shorty and Biff? Sure. They're along. Dippy was scared an' wouldn't come. But I knew you was regular so when you went out me'n Shorty brought you 'long seein' you wasn't hurt bad. Glad, huh?"

"How 'e be glad when you ain't tell 'eem!'"

Fallon laughed. "S'right, Biff. Here I'm thinkin' the kid knows all about it." He leaned over Skippy again: "I didn't have no chance puttin' you wise on the way up an' I go an' forget you been out cold since we hit the ditch."

Skippy felt a chill up and down his spine at this reminder. "We hit somethin'—so it was a ditch, huh? Gee! I got hurt then, huh?"

"Yeah," Fallon replied laconically, "but not's bad as them bulls. The three hadda take it—the driver couldn't put up no fight. Dippy was bruised too, but not so bad but what he could say no when we told him he could come with us an' beat his rap. So Barker says not to bother 'cause there wasn't no time for arguin' an' another car might come along."

"Barker—Frost—" Skippy asked puzzled, "they're your friends, huh?"

"*Friends!* I'll say so! Cheese, ain't it a friend that gets us away so easy as this? Lissen, kid—it shows how friendly when I'm waitin' in the cooler this afternoon an' along comes this Frost an' he says he gets in by sayin' he's my cousin comin' to say so-long. Then he says how he heard the long stretch they gimme an' that he don't think they gimme no break. So then he talks like a Dutch uncle an' says how he an' his pal Barker can give us a break. We don't do nothin' he says. Him an' Barker'll find out somehow what time we're gonna take the ride to the jug. An' they do."

"Oh!" Skippy groaned as the car bumped his head painfully.

"Feelin' all right, kid?" Fallon asked sympathetically.

"Yeah," Skippy answered half-heartedly. "It's just the bumps that make my head ache."

"We'll soon be there," called the sonorous voice which Skippy recognized as Barker's.

He raised himself painfully from Fallon's accommodating lap and sat upright in the seat. The Greek named Biff was sitting on his left and on the end of the seat sat his partner Shorty. Both were smiling at him anxiously, particularly Biff who had a rather set mirthfulness in his round face.

Fallon obligingly crowded himself into the other corner of the back seat in order to give Skippy plenty of room. "Anyways, you must be feelin' a little better wantin' to sit up," he said peering over at him. Suddenly he lowered his voice and whispered, "Say, kid, we ain't gotta worry now 'cause Barker an' Frost's gonna see us through an' how! Look what chances Frost took!"

"What?" Skippy inquired, aware that a feeling of foreboding had taken possession of him.

"*Chances?*" Fallon continued hoarsely. "Didn't he find out from one of them guards what time we was leavin' an' didn't he hang 'round the court house till he sees the bulls' car drive up!"

"Gee!" Skippy said, feeling incapable of saying anything more.

"Sure! So like I'm sayin', Frost waits his time an' he goes an' gets talkin' to the driver indifferent like. It's the same driver of the car we come up in—see?"

Skippy was beginning to see only too well, but he did not say so.

"Anyways, the driver says after a while he better go in an' see if they're set with the kids. Frost says sure, so long. He's dressed in overalls like a mechanic—see? When the driver goes in the building, Flint quick opens the hood an' shoots some stuff what he's got in his pocket, in the oil. Jest enough so's to make it get workin' by the time we hit the bumpy road—see?"

Skippy stared.

"Well, there ain't much more. Frost strolls 'round the corner an' he quick gets in this car with Barker sittin' there like he is now. It's a cinch! They start off ahead 'cause the driver's already told Frost what road he takes for Delafield. They wait behind some trees down that bumpy road an' when we blow along they give us a coupla hunnerd feet ahead an' follow without no lights. So when the engine goes bad on the driver an' we hit the ditch, it's more'n Frost an' Barker expect."

"Yeah," Frost spoke up in a loud, raucous voice. "We expected they'd be stalled and standin' around lookin' for help so that when we cruised up soft and easy with no lights on, it'd be a cinch to cover the bulls and get Fallon and whoever of you kids that wanted to scram, into our car. But so help me, it was easier than that!"

"Yeah," Fallon echoed, seeming to enjoy his role as narrator. "When Frost and Barker come along, there we was ditched—the bulls knocked silly an' the driver so goofy it was a cinch for Frost to stick him up and knock him cold when he tries to keep us from scrammin'."

"Frost used a gun, eh?"

"Sure! But he didn't have to shoot. An' then that sap Donovan kid wouldn't come when he had that break. He said we'd be caught an' we'd get a worse stretch. Aw, he was just yeller! Anyways, it was lucky that us guys didn't get it like the bulls. Only you was out, kid. Well, we're on our way, so we should worry, hah?"

"Where we goin'?" Skippy asked as calmly as he could.

Frost and Barker were deep in some conversation of their own and seemed to be paying no attention to their charges. Fallon leaned close to Skippy's ear and whispered, "Between you an' me, kid, I think it's a hideout Barker's got somewhere in the country. We been ridin' an hour now. Barker's boss—see? I think he's done a coupla stretches hisself 'cause Frost told me on the Q. T. that Barker's got feelin' for kids that get a break like we got an' so he helps 'em crash out whenever he can. He's gonna keep us under cover awhile till things quiet down an' then he's gonna get us out west to some friends. I ain't s'posed ta tell though. Frost says Barker wants to s'prise us."

"And you say Frost—Barker's your friend too, huh?" Skippy asked timidly. "You known 'em long, huh Fallon?"

"Nah," Nickie answered readily. "I ain't never laid eyes on Frost till in the cooler this afternoon." And in a hushed voice, he added: "I ain't had no good look at Barker yet, ridin' like we are without no lights. I first hear his voice when I get in this car—he just waited for us when he sees how things was. We should worry when we got friends like them?"

Friends! Skippy put his hand to his head, hoping for the best, but fearing the worst.

CHAPTER VII

THE HOUSE FORGOTTEN

The question pounded in his head more insistently than the pain he was suffering. Did not this whole unlooked-for episode of Frost and Barker smack too much of Dean Devlin's tactics? And could it not be possible that Devlin might change not only his name but his tactics also? After all, he concluded, it was but a step from Barker to Devlin and from the Delafield Reformatory to the Juvenile Court. The man Devlin that Carlton Conne had told him about was certainly clever enough to keep a step ahead of the police every time.

Skippy felt more hopeless about it all as the minutes sped by. Here they were going farther and farther away—heaven only knew where; and, though he was aware that due to the accident, Mr. Conne could not but think him blameless, he felt that in a measure he had failed. He hadn't any business, he told himself, to strike his head and fall unconscious—it was his job to *stay* conscious!

A DINGY SQUARE ROOFED HOUSE LOOMED UP BEFORE
THEM.

The fact that Dorcas, a trusted and experienced detective, had also been knocked senseless seemed not to lessen this feeling of guilt. Skippy was steeped in remorse because an unkind Fate had seen fit to have Fallon carry him away from Dorcas' side, away from the influence that was Mr. Conne's and which spelled safety to him.

And yet, at that moment, he was not afraid, notwithstanding the fact that he felt that Barker and Dean Devlin might be the same person. He was merely puzzled as to how he should get word to Mr. Conne if it was going to be as Fallon said, that Barker would keep them under cover for a month.

He decided that he was feeling too sick to worry about it yet. He longed only to get in a bed and sleep and let the morrow take care of itself. And if Barker proved to be Devlin, he could only hope that Fortune would smile upon him and help him to succeed despite the mischance that had cut him off from Mr. Conne's help and the International offices.

A long silence prevailed in the car. Shorty and Biff were sound asleep on each other's shoulders and emitting soft nasal sounds. Nickie Fallon was hunched in his corner in a half doze and up in front Frost and Barker were deep in whispered conversation.

The road was rough but Frost handled the car expertly, driving it as if he knew the bad spots by experience. He had only his parking lights on now and they were speeding along with surprisingly little sound from the engine.

After a time they entered a narrow, wooded lane and Frost seemed to pick his way more carefully. Skippy was quick to note that the trees, in places, interlaced and during their entire journey through that section, one could stretch one's arms at either side and touch the overhanging branches. For at least an hour, he guessed, they hadn't passed a house.

"We come up back roads, I betcha," Nickie Fallon whispered suddenly as if guessing his thoughts. "Looks like we're miles from nowhere. This guy Barker knows his hide-outs, hah?"

"Mm," said Skippy. "Gee, we wouldn't know howta get back home if we wanted to, huh?"

"Frost says we can't an' what's more we ain't to try, in case we get thinkin' we're smarter than him or Barker is. He says kids like us 'ud run right into the bulls an' that 'ud make it bad for them—see? Him an' Barker'd do a long stretch if we squealed that they helped us crash. So Frost says they ain't takin' no chances on lettin' us think we can get anywheres alone. They're gonna treat us swell s'long as we're stickin' under cover till they help us go west. So we gotta get used to stayin' quiet a little while—see?"

"Yeah," Skippy answered, "I think so." He could feel Nickie Fallon looking at him curiously. Suddenly he felt the boy move closer to him.

"Say, lissen, kid," he whispered, "d'you feel funny 'bout this Frost an' Baker?"

"Gee," said Skippy, not a little startled, "I—I dunno.... I—whadda you mean, huh?"

Fallon's lips almost touched Skippy's ear. "Listen kid," he confided, "I ain't been doin' what I done, an' not learnin' that guys don't do nothin' for love. How come, they been takin' all this trouble for some kids they ain't never laid eyes on 'fore today, hah?"

"Whadda you s'pose?" Skippy whispered timidly.

"We ain't tippin' off Shorty or Biff, but between you'n me, kid, I think these guys got some job for us what they can't do themselves—see? A little job, mebbe."

"Yeah, an' if they have, it's all right, huh?" Skippy retorted making a brave effort to measure up as one of Nickie's kind.

"Sure, only if it's bigger'n we can do an' we get grabbed—we're outa luck. That'd mean double time. Aw, it ain't no use worryin'. If they let us put the feed bag on regular an' give us bunks, it's worth doin' 'em a favor."

Skippy nodded but did not answer. He was too intent on watching the number of turns that Frost had made within the past few moments. They had already made three off the wooded road and now with the fourth one they were in a dense woods and proceeding very slowly along a road little wider than a footpath. Then suddenly they rolled into a clearing and stopped. Frost chuckled and switched on his headlights.

A house, square-roofed and dingy, loomed up before them. Its shingles were so devoid of paint that it was impossible to say what color they had originally been painted. Blistered and peeling from long years of neglect and with its shutters closed like so many pairs of sleeping eyes the structure presented a picture of abject loneliness.

Unkempt grass and weeds grew up to the high stoop; there was no porch. Behind the house and a little to the left, Skippy glimpsed a barn that was also in disrepair. Notwithstanding this, he supposed that Barker and Frost parked their car in it.

"No bulls'll turn you kids up here," Frost said, as if reading their thoughts. He turned a leathern-looking face toward Skippy, smiling out of shrewd eyes. "This house usta be in the center of a village till a fire burned the town out. Then the railroad decided to run twenty-five miles away so the folks left it flat. This bein' the only house left they let the woods grow up 'round it and now, after seventy-five years, nobody knew about it, 'cept an old nit-wit hermit that put me and Barker wise. Last year he died so there ain't nobody now'll bother you kids, much less the bulls."

Barker turned to them and in the half-light his long, grave face and staring light eyes contrasted strangely with the dark wisps of hair that straggled from under his hat and down on his forehead. But it was when he talked that Skippy was startled, for the man's voice was so solemn and sonorous that it was eerie.

"Now boys," he was saying, "you see how safe you are here. Keep it in mind and don't get the idea that you can manage your own freedom better than I can. For one thing, it would get Frost and me into trouble if you were picked up and if you weren't, you'd get in trouble yourselves, because this place is almost all surrounded by swamps and you might not find your way out. When I say the coast is clear to ship you west—all right. You'll come out of this house then, and not before!"

There was a warning note in his voice that sent a chill up and down Skippy's spine. He wished his Airedale, Mugs, had lived to be with him at a time like this. Shorty and Biff exchanged a few words in their native tongue and suddenly Nickie Fallon's hand stole over and coming in contact with Skippy's wrist, he grasped it tightly.

CHAPTER VIII

TIMMY

Even from the outside one could sense the desolation of the house. It took little imagination to visualize the large, sprawling rooms downstairs and the small, stuffy rooms upstairs weighted down to a point of suffocation by the flat tin roof. Cobwebs, slugs, every scurrying, every crawling thing that thrived in dampness and gloom must thrive in such a place, Skippy thought.

He was glad of Nickie Fallon's friendly hand on his arm as they ascended the high stoop. And he was considerably cheered by the oily, smiling faces of Shorty and Biff as they all followed in the wake of the two men. He had somehow forgotten that these three lawless boys would have been repugnant to him under other conditions. Now he welcomed them as old companions, and their nearness was comforting in this chill, lonely moment.

"Metal doors 'n everythin'," Nickie whispered in his ear. "Locks outside too, hah? What's out is out an' what's in is in!"

They entered a stuffy vestibule and passed into a long, dark hall. At the far end of it beside the stairway was a lantern standing on a broken stool. It gave a feeble light at best, but now it sputtered and flickered like some dying thing and sent out weird shadows that stole up and down the dirty walls.

Barker stood a moment as if listening. Then he turned his grave face to Frost and said, "No sound from upstairs. Timmy must be asleep. Go up and get him. We'll make some coffee and have something to eat. When you come down put some oil in that lantern."

Skippy wondered who Timmy was, but soon dismissed the thought in his joy at hearing that they would get something to eat. Nickie, too, brightened up at this announcement and Shorty and Biff made no secret of their delight, but gave vent to several nasal grunts.

Frost hurried back and ascended the narrow, rickety stairway two steps at a time. Barker motioned the boys into a room at his right where he already had a lantern lighted.

"Sit down," he said abruptly. "I'm going out to the kitchen to make coffee." Then, without having really looked at them, he stepped into the hall. There was the sound of a key turning in the door outside and suddenly he was back again, passing through the room and toward another door as if he didn't know the boys were there. When that door had closed behind him, his footsteps could be heard echoing over bare boards, until, after other doors slammed, there ensued a few moments of silence.

Skippy had taken a chair like the rest and now he glanced around the big room. Besides the chairs they were occupying there were two other chairs standing, battered and forlorn, against the shuttered and heavily barred windows. The room boasted no other furniture and no rugs; the floor was thick with dust.

"Well, it's good there ain't no more furniture to catch the dust, hah?" Fallon commented humorously as he took note of their surroundings. "Say, I wonder what's the big idea, barrin' windows—I ain't keen on bars. Makes me think we're in Delafield almost."

Shorty got up softly and moved his chair close to the others. When his pudgy body was seated, he leaned over confidentially and said, "Mebbe we better in Delafield, eh Neecky?" He shook his round head at his friend Biff, then nodded back at Fallon. "Eet look what ya call phoney the way thees Barker don' look at us an' how he bring us here to thees spooky, dirty place, eh?"

"Just what I teenck!" Biff agreed in an undertone. "I get dem creeps—you know? Ever'ting eet should be fun eef Barker an' Frost fool dem bulls an' take us keeds from de school—eet should be fun eef they do it because they no want us to do the stretch and feel dis seempathy, eh? But no—they act like we was goin' to funeral, yes Neecky?"

"Aw, forget it!" Nicky answered. "I'll admit I ain't got no yen for this joint myself. But we ain't where we can say we'd like a nice up-to-date apartment. We gotta be glad we ain't startin' no long stretch at Delafield. I got a hunch Frost's kinda slippery an' Barker's a queer bird all right, but what's that when they're keepin' us outa the hoosegow!"

"An' for thees, Neecky—what we do, eh?" Biff asked, squinting his small, brown eyes.

"I think," Nicky whispered, "they got a small job for us guys to do—see? Ain't we all done a job or two for ourselves, hah? So we can do a job for them if they ast us—see?" He turned to Skippy suddenly and asked, "Ain't that right, kid?"

"Sure!" Skippy answered, conscious of an inward tremor as he said it.

"That's the kind of talk I like to hear, boys!" came a sepulchral voice from the doorway where Barker stood watching them. He was grave and unsmiling, and save for a certain steely glint in his staring eyes, his face looked not unlike a cold, clay mask.

Nickie Fallon broke the tension with a forced, husky laugh. "You'n Frost give us a break, Mr. Barker," he said nervously, "we'd be short skates if we didn't try an' square it."

"Of course," Barker agreed without any enthusiasm.

A silence ensued that to Skippy was tense. Barker continued to stand there and stare, and the boys sat rigid in their chairs until the welcome sound of footsteps was heard coming down the stairs and along the hall.

Frost strode into the big room and in his wake was a tall, fair-haired boy of about sixteen whose appearance was somewhat disheveled. He had a wild expression in his light blue eyes and at sight of Barker a shadow crossed his face.

"I been most crazy barred up in that dark hole since daylight!" he cried. "I thought you'n Frost would never come! Honest, I'll go nuts if I ain't let out soon. Over a month an' two kids're gone an' I'm still here! Barker, it's givin' me the creeps—honest! It's worse'n if I stayed in the pen up in Al...."

"I've arranged for you to go tomorrow night, Timmy," Barker interposed hastily. And, nodding his long head toward the new arrivals, he added: "You'll have these boys to keep you company till then."

Timmy wheeled about, obviously unaware of the boys' presence in the room until that moment. He drew a hand across his forehead as if dazed. Then suddenly, in a trembling voice, he said, "More!"

Skippy felt himself trembling too.

CHAPTER IX

TRAPPED

Skippy was destined to remember that night. Whether it was the chill gloom of the house or the nameless dread which seemed to hang like a pall over the wilderness hideout, he did not know. Certainly, everything they said and did gave them a feeling of unreality, as if they were merely moving puppets in a play. He missed his father, as he never had before, and that was saying much.

After their peculiar meeting with Timmy Brogan (as they afterward learned was his full name), Barker gravely invited them to the kitchen for refreshment. They followed Frost through two unfurnished rooms, wading through the dirt and dark until they emerged into a sprawling room running the width of the house and which, like the sitting room, was illuminated by means of a lantern dangling from a hook in the high ceiling.

A small oil stove, battered and rusty, was trying to send up a yellow flame strong enough to boil the coffee. Another stove, a wood-burner, stood back in the opposite corner as if it were trying to hide its antiquity from the boys' eyes. A sprawling cupboard stood in another corner and in the center of the room, surrounded by broken down chairs and boxes, was a dilapidated table holding several plates of freshly-made sandwiches.

"Sit down, boys," Barker said simply. "The coffee will be ready in a minute."

"Seems like I ain't fed in a million minutes!" Timmy said with bitter complaint. "Since you left me that lousy sandwich when you beat it at dawn, I...."

"*Shut up!*"

Barker's funereal voice filled the room for a tense second, then he turned on his heel and walked toward the cupboard in long, determined strides. Timmy grew pale and sat down on the nearest box, reaching hungrily for a sandwich.

Frost chuckled mirthlessly for no reason at all that Skippy could see. Barker took out several thick cups with which he strode back toward the stove and poured the coffee when it was ready. After that they ate, and a strange, silent repast it was with the lantern sending eerie shadows up on the smoke-blackened ceiling and leaving the little group in a semi-gloom about the table.

Skippy ate because he was hungry, but his mind wasn't on it. He was too confused, too worried at the unexpected turn of events to think of anything else but what had happened and what might happen. Barker made him feel strangely hopeless about this adventure which he had set out upon so light heartedly and which Carlton Conne had seemed to plan so thoroughly. It now appeared that he who had planned on helping to trap Dean Devlin had himself been trapped in a larger web.

That was it—he was *trapped*!

He looked at the two kitchen windows. They were shuttered and barred like the windows in the other rooms. The door leading out of the kitchen opened onto a shed and Skippy was certain that that too was invulnerable both inside and out. Upstairs, he learned ten minutes later, were three stuffy bedrooms fit for occupation. He was assigned to one of them along with Nickie Fallon and Timmy. Shorty and Biff occupied the room next to them and across the hall was the room in which Barker and Frost alternately slept and watched to see that their young protégés did not triumph over locks and other man-made obstructions and steal forth into the night.

"Ever since I been here, I been askin' myself—why the locks, if them two guys brought me here outa sympathy?" Timmy whispered to his new room-mates as Frost bade them a chuckling good-night and locked the door on the outside. He retreated to his tumbled looking cot and held his head in his hands wearily while he stared at the lantern hanging above his head. "Take it from me, guys, there's somethin' screwy about Barker an' Frost, an' you might's well get smarted up."

Skippy looked at the decrepit bed in which he and Nickie were to sleep and his heart sank. There wasn't a breath of air save the occasional wisps of breeze that mysteriously found their way through the chinks in the shutters. He walked to the window and by stooping could look through the bars and see a rising moon casting a flickering gleam of light on water.

"Is it a lake or somethin'?" he asked.

"Lake, me eye!" Timmy answered. "It's a swamp, that's what. You'll see how much when the moon comes up good. There's only a little back yard an' then the swamp begins."

"Say," Nickie whispered inquiringly, "you got somepin' on Barker an' Frost? What's the matter, anyways?"

Timmy got up and walked over to Fallon. "They got me scared, that's what! Barker's terrible—he's got me scared skinny an' I'll tell you guys why!" He tiptoed to the door, listened a moment and then came back. "Did *he* help you guys crash outa reform?"

Nickie explained that they had not got that far before Barker had reached out a helping hand and gathered them in. While he was speaking they all moved toward the bed and sat down, there being no chairs in the room.

"So he kinda switched the deck with you guys for a change, hah?" Timmy commented after Fallon finished. "That proves what I say about him bein' a pretty foxy guy, turnin' a trick that maybe ain't gonna be so healthy for us in the end."

"How come?" Skippy asked softly.

"It's a long story, an' if you guys ain't sleepy..." Timmy began.

"Say, lissen," Nickie interposed, "the kid'n me don't mind bein' put hip. I didn't like the way Barker bore down on you downstairs an' it give me the hunch mebbe he's too phoney even for us—see! So come across an' mebbe we won't get the short enda the stick."

"Sure I'll spiel, but that's all the good it'll do," Timmy said dismally. "We'll never get nowheres together, take it from me—Barker ain't lettin' us! He'll take us away from here, one by one, and so far the two guys that have gone from here ... anyways, I'll tell you what I think—Barker's a *killer!*"

"*What?*" Skippy gulped.

They heard the scraping of a lock and suddenly the door swung open. A breeze from the hall blew out the feeble lantern light and they were in total darkness.

CHAPTER X

THE WAY OF DEVLIN

Skippy felt Nickie's hand on his arm and Timmy crowded up close to both of them. For a second there was no sound, then they heard someone move in the doorway and presently Barker's voice pierced the darkness.

"What have you been whispering about in here, Timmy?" he demanded.

"*Whisperin'?*" Timmy's voice trembled ever so little. "Aw, I was only tellin' these guys how you got me outa the pen an' they was tellin' me how slick you helped them—that's all."

Skippy was certain that Barker sighed. In any event, he said, "Hmph! You better let them go to sleep and do your talking tomorrow!" He shut the door as swiftly as he had opened it—the key turned in the lock and all was silence.

Nickie was alert, tense. He nudged Skippy and Timmy and then he moved his lips. "Us three can cram into bed," he said so softly that the boys had to strain their ears to hear. "We'll pull a blanket over our heads so's we can talk—see? It'll be hot, but we should worry, hah?"

Skippy was worried, but he didn't say so for he, too, was anxious to learn from Timmy what lay behind Barker's grave, almost brooding exterior. He undressed and hopped in on one side of Timmy while Nickie crawled in on the other and if they felt stifled as they whispered under the blanket for three-quarters of an hour or more, they were not aware of it, so intensely interesting was the story to which they were listening.

"Where do I come from?" Timmy repeated in answer to Skippy's question. "Albany. Barker comes in the jug where I'm doin' five years—for stealin'. Well, he looks like a minister an' I think he passes it out that he is one. Anyway, he spies me an' gets talkin' kinda religious an' fatherly while the guard's around. When the bloke strolls off, Barker quick drops the fatherly act an' wants to know would I like to crash. Sure, I tells him. He tells me to be set the next night—that he'll be waitin'. When he leaves he slips me fifty bucks an' tells me to slip it to the guard I think'll look the other way for that much jack."

"You made it, huh?" Skippy asked.

"Easy. Fifty bucks is big money for them guards. The one I stake lets me slip without no trouble at all. Barker was waitin' outside in a big closed car."

"Frost with him?" Skippy asked curiously.

"Nope. I never seen that grinnin' skunk till Barker brings me down to this hole. That's a month an' a half ago. Barker took me straight to a house in Albany where he said he rented a room. On the way he tells me that from then on I should say I'm his son. So I do. We only stay in the house three days. I'm willin' to keep under cover so he tells the landlady an' everybody I ain't feelin' so well, that's the reason I don't go out. Barker steps out plenty an' I hear him talkin' to the landlady down the hall."

"What'd they talk about?" Skippy asked.

"Sure—it was nothin' much. A lotta boloney! Barker makes the dame think he's one grand old man—all for his wild son—all that bunk. Anyways, the last day we're there he drags me out right after dark. Takes me to a doctor. When I ast him what for, he says that's his business; that I should act like a sulky son. Well, I do it. The doc gimme the up an' down an' says O. K. So we go back to the house an' the landlady hands Barker a telegram that I found out afterward was from Frost. It says somethin' about grandma bein' sick; that he should come home to New York. It was signed Joe."

"Then you packed up an' come here, I bet," Skippy said.

"Sure," Timmy murmured. "He leaves the telegram on the bureau an' down in the hall he gives the landlady a coupla weeks' rent. Tells her if we ain't back by then, he'll send the dough every week till we do get back. He give her a song and dance bout wantin' a farm when he come back an' that he wanted the room to come back to so's he'd have a place while he was lookin'. When we come away he tells me it's a lotta boloney he give her; that he only wanted the room till this little business broke O. K. He says he ain't got no idea of goin' back there."

"Mm," said Nickie, "sounds like he was buildin' an alibi for hisself, hah?"

"That's what I gets thinkin'," Timmy admitted. "Anyways, we ride all night an' plenty next mornin' till we hit a woods in the mountains where Barker parked his car way in the trees. We slep' there all afternoon, then start ridin' again when the sun was goin' down. Bout nine or so we come here. Frost's here. So's two kids bout our age—Willie Meehan, an' Sammie Brown. Next day we get comparin' things—Willie comes from Boston an' Sammie from Syracuse. They crashed jugs like me, with Barker's help. What's more they all stayed in a city room a coupla days like me an' just before they leave a telegram comes tellin' Barker he's gotta hustle to New York on business or that old stuff bout his dying grandmother. Anyways it's Frost that always sends 'em."

"An' those kids," Skippy asked eagerly, "did they say they were Barker's sons an' go to a doctor like you?"

"Sure. It's the same old line—he'll do the same with you guys too. Blamed if I know his racket, but when I'm here about a week, Willie says Barker's sendin' him west that night. Willie's here a little over a month then. Seems he don't keep kids much longer'n that—I'm overdue now!" He laughed grimly. "Anyways, he beats it with Willie an' we was glad he was gettin' a break an' on his way. So two days after Barker comes back—it's at night like he always comes an' goes an' Sammy an' me's sleepin' in this room. Frost and Barker think we're dead's doornails so when they come upstairs they get arguin' an' forget how loud they talk. Well, I'm awake and how! I hear the whole works."

"*Gee!*" Skippy breathed, happy in the thought that now perhaps he would learn something of value to Mr. Conne, when he should be so fortunate as to see the detective again.

"Yeah, I said a lotta things like that when I was listening," Timmy confided. "I heard Barker say somethin' about that Willie wouldn't go through. So Frost asks him what he did then. Barker says he had to do the job hisself. Frost laughs when he hears that. He tells Devlin he better plan his jobs better if he don't wanta take the hot squat."

"*Devlin?*" Skippy asked breathlessly.

"Yeah, I forgot to tell—Barker's an alias. Devlin's his right moniker. I found it out when I was here two days."

"So Frost told him he might burn?" Nickie asked, as if he was turning this odd warning over in his mind. "And that's what makes you think Barker's a killer—'cause Frost cracked that?"

"Yeah—sure. What else? Sammy promised he'd try an' get word back to me somehow so's to lemme know what job Barker wanted him to do, but he knew an' I knew it couldn't be done. Barker'd most likely send him too far away afterward. He went a coupla weeks ago. I been alone since, wonderin' an' worryin' when my turn'd come an' what it'd be!" Timmy took a deep breath and almost sobbed. "If it's a killin' job—I ain't goin' through. I ain't gonna pull no trigger on nobody for Barker or nobody else!"

"Me, neither!" Nickie asserted flatly. "Looks like Barker springs us 'cause it's easier than springin' older guys in the big house. Then he gets us for a job an' if anybody's grabbed it'll be us 'cause the law figures us future criminals anyway—see? Ten to one he dopes it we won't squeal 'cause he's did us a favor."

"Just what *I* think!" Timmy agreed.

Not having the lawless squint upon such matters, Skippy did not know what to think. His active mind was full of plausible answers to the problem, yet somehow he could find no convincing explanation as to Devlin's real motive. Why did the man, in each case, hire a room and have the boy pose as his son? Why was each boy required to go with him to a physician? There seemed no answer to those questions. Particularly was he puzzled as to why Devlin should accord them all this prisoner-like treatment while they were awaiting release.

He got nowhere along this line. He always ended by asking himself the question: was Devlin as grim of soul as he was of features? Some inner voice was ever prompt in answering this query of his and it was always the same.

Yes!

CHAPTER XI

OVERHEARD

Sleep wouldn't come to Skippy that night. Hours after Timmy had dejectedly gone to his cot and Nickie had sunk into deep, untroubled slumber beside him, he lay on the hot bed worried and lonely. Aunt Min and Carlton Conne seemed separated from him by a dark and terrible abyss, and he shivered with the fear that he might not get back again to the people and places that typified law, order and safety. Particularly safety.

He hadn't any illusions now. Clearly, nothing but a miracle would get him out of the web which had so entangled him the moment he had been placed in Dean Devlin's car. Nothing save an almost impossible combination of favorable circumstances would make it possible for him to get word to Mr. Conne. And how, if it were true that Devlin kept them imprisoned until he saw fit to embark them on the dark, mysterious "job," could those circumstances occur so that he might be of any real help to Carlton Conne? He despaired of any such good fortune.

The breeze was not strong enough to penetrate through the shuttered window now. Nothing but damp, humid heat found its way to his burning cheeks. He felt the stillness about the air augured a heavy storm and soon he heard thunder in the distance.

The buzz of crickets, the tin-like sound of locusts vied with the deep throated chorus of frogs about the house. Once an owl lent its eerie hoot to this droning night symphony and, as if in answer, another chorus of insects filled the air with dismal chantings.

Skippy stood it as long as he could, then got up and tiptoed to the window to get a breath of air. Through the bars he could see the quarter moon, a shimmering bit of silver light gleaming upon the swamp and here and there transforming it into pools of shining, black lacquer. Overhead, however, sullen clouds were slowly trespassing and it would be only minutes before the lonely place would be surrounded by darkness and storm.

He clung to one of the bars and peered down upon the roof of the woodshed just below the window. It would be an easy jump down there, he decided—easy, if it were not for the five long strips of iron that so effectually barred the way. Crude and amateurish though they looked, Skippy knew that they had been put there to withstand any such feeble attacks as his two bare hands might make upon them.

While he was digesting this fact he became aware of voices, Frost's and Devlin's, coming from the hall. He stepped toward the door noiselessly and pressed his ear close against it.

The men were not in the hall as he had at first thought, they were in their room with the door ajar. It was evident that they had intended to converse in whispers, but presently they were launched upon an argument and caution was forgotten.

"Tell me if you can," Devlin was saying angrily, "what I'm going to do with those two Greeks, eh? It isn't enough that you didn't discover what they were before we brought them all the way here, but on top of it, you tell me I'll think of what to do about them! *I'll think*, eh?" He sneered. "All I can think of is that they're Greeks and that I don't look anything like a Greek or talk anything like one! How can I pass them off as my sons, eh?"

"Easy, boss, easy," Frost said placatingly, "I didn't know they was Greeks no more'n you. They was sentenced before I gets into court. The ones I counted on was that Nickie and that other kid, Dippy and that smart-looking youngster John Doe. You coulda knocked me cold with a feather when Fallon tags the Greeks along. There wasn't no time to argue, was there?"

"All right—all right," Devlin boomed. "Just tell me what I'm going to do with 'em! They can't go back and tell what they've seen here and I'm not going to go to the trouble of getting them off my hands without getting some money out of it, that's all there is to it!"

"O. K., boss. It's soft—soft." Frost's voice was rasping yet servile. "There's black wigs a guy can buy, ain't there? Well, I'll grab me one, fix myself up like a grease ball, talk spig, take the kids one at a time and try my hand at your racket."

"Now you're talking, Frost. Take one—say, to Pittsburgh, eh? You'll be father and son looking for work in the mills. And I'd only aim for the minimum price on both of them. They're not worth taking any chances on big money. The other Greek you could take—say to Maine. That's putting a safe distance between, eh?"

"Sure thing, boss," Frost crowed. "And say, listen, why not lemme clean up the job right on the spot, hey? No use makin' extra trips back here. I can work it careful."

"Hmp—it's an idea, Frost. We'll dope it out after tomorrow night and Timmy's off my mind. Don't try to do anything until then." There was a pause, then: "Do you think he's wise to anything? I sort of feel that he was doing more than just whisper his family history to those other kids."

"Nah; what could he say, hey? He ain't seen nothin' no more'n the others. You're just gettin' nervous, that's all. But I'll tell you what, Dean, you *will* make them kids wise that something's phoney with your big heart racket, when you don't even trust 'em unless you got the key to their room in your pocket. You're puttin' the lid flat down and scarin' the life out of 'em too soon. Now if I was you, I'd let 'em loose in the house. Maybe if you'd done that in Chi, Tucker wouldn't got away like he done. If he'd known where you hung out he'd been back and you'd cashed in on him."

"Well, I didn't and that's my funeral," Devlin said in measured tones. "I'm only glad Tucker wasn't caught so he could spill out my racket. I guess he got away all right or we'd have seen some flat-footed dick keeping our trail warm before this. Anyway, I think you're right about locking up the kids. I'll make 'em think I trust 'em even if I don't."

"O. K.," Frost chuckled, "I'll do it right now and give 'em a surprise in the morning. Long's I got the keys to the downstairs doors in my pockets, we ain't got no cause to worry that they'll sneak."

Skippy did not wait to hear more. He made a running jump from the door to the bed and had assumed a restful, sleeping posture before Frost's key scraped in the lock. But the man made no effort to enter. Instead, he turned on his heel and recrossed the hall to his room and presently a deep silence pervaded the house.

Not many seconds later, the storm broke and the dark, eerie house trembled and groaned like some stricken thing in the whistling gale.

CHAPTER XII

THE STORM

Rain lashed against the shutters and poured down the side of the house in torrents. Loose shingles slammed and clattered with every twist of the wind and the trees bowing down before its fury moaned piteously, their branches squeaking and crackling like ancient spectral voices in the night.

A zig-zag streak of lightning flashed upon the dirty wall and the clap of thunder that followed seemed to sweep away all rational thought. To Skippy, the world had suddenly gone mad and he did not wonder at it since Devlin, asleep no doubt, had locked within his black heart secrets which challenged even the warring elements.

Carlton Conne had said of Devlin that he was criminal, but not dangerously so. Perhaps that had been true once, but not now. Devlin had contributed something more than just law evasion to the sordid atmosphere of the house. Human laws defied had given the place its dark, furtive character for one sensed it in every nook and corner that made up the tottering structure.

The storm screamed on and through the tiny, hot room a cooling breeze now found its way. Skippy shifted around to the foot of the bed and let the welcome air blow over him. He wished he might call out and hear a cheery answer from Big Joe Tully as in the old river days. Nickie was still undisturbed by the shrieking night and Timmy, though restless and tossing about, was asleep.

Skippy thought of the two Greeks, Shorty and Biff, apparently oblivious of the meaning of it all. Their bland, oily faces reflected pretty accurately the stupid squint which they had on their petty thieving practices; it was the only thing they knew, the only means of living which they could understand. Skippy wondered how they would feel about the dark and seemingly sinister "job" which Devlin or Frost would demand that they carry out as the price for their sympathetic "protection."

Not for a moment was Skippy deceived as to who was the brains of the Devlin-Frost combination. Frost was a chuckling, subservient thief, but it was in the depths of Dean Devlin's dubious soul that the plans were carefully laid.

He was making mental note of all these things in anticipation of the day when he should see Carlton Conne and give his report. It made not a bit of difference that this day now seemed remote—it had to come sometime! He would spend all his waking hours preparing for it despite the bars and locked doors that mocked him.

He would escape somehow—some day!

The sound of scurrying rats overhead gave him a brilliant idea. The attic! Was that barred also? He determined to find out somehow, now that Frost had so generously secured for them the run of the house. Well, he would run, certainly, just as soon as the opportunity presented itself.

As he meditated he heard Timmy throw himself from the cot and shriek. Skippy was on his feet and helping him up in a second.

"Dreaming—huh, Timmy?"

Timmy was trembling violently. "It was like as if it was true," he said in a choking voice. "I'm dreamin' it's a night like this an' I'm out with Devlin in a funny-lookin' old car."

"Aw, it's this storm what made you dream," Nickie interposed, aroused by the commotion and sitting up rubbing his eyes.

Timmy's protest was almost a sob. "I'm tellin' you it was real-like! We're ridin' along in the dark an' it's lightnin' an' I'm gettin' wet an' I shiver. All of a sudden it don't look like Devlin sittin' beside me no more—it's like a ghost without no body—just big, starin' eyes like Devlin's—then I'm wise he's a killer—see? But he's gonna kill *me*!" Timmy crawled up on his cot and sat down, still trembling. "Somehow I don't remember what happened after that till I feel like I'm runnin' an' that Devlin's chasin' me. Then when I feel like I'm half dead I look up an' see it's this house. Up in the attic I see you an' Nickie at the little window. I'm hurt an' tell how Devlin tries to kill me. All of a sudden long arms come reachin' out from behind a big tree out in front. All I see is Devlin's starin' eyes an' I'm sorta chokin' to death when I wake up on the floor."

"Holy Smoke!" Nickie exclaimed. "What a guy! Can't you pick out nothin' better to dream about?"

Skippy sat down beside Timmy and patted him sympathetically. Suddenly the door opened and they saw Devlin's tall form outlined there.

"What's going on here?" he asked impatiently.

"Timmy," Skippy ventured; "he's hadda bad dream an' it threw him outa bed!"

"Hmph!" the man boomed in his funereal voice. "Dreams don't come true! Get back to bed and to sleep, you kids!" He shut the door and they heard his bare feet patter across the hall.

Nickie sneered contemptuously at the door. "It'd be too bad for you, Devlin, if that dream did come true!"

"But it won't," Skippy said soothingly. "My aunt always says dreams are always opposite."

Timmy had got hold of himself somewhat, and valiantly tried to forget his dream. "Yep," he agreed, "I guess that's right. Mebbe it was the heat an' my stomach. I never could eat right fore goin' to bed without dreamin' terrible things. But I never dreamed nothin' bad's that, that's all." He laughed nervously. "Aw, I'll forget it!"

Skippy wondered if he really would. Somehow he had the feeling that he wouldn't forget it—not ever!

CHAPTER XIII

THE EVERGREEN TREE

The remainder of the night was a torment. Toward dawn Skippy dozed occasionally only to awaken each time with a start to find himself trembling and expectant. What he might hear or see he could not imagine, but he watched with relief the murky light of the new day seeping in through the chinks of the shutter and routing the dismal gloom that kept him in breathless suspense.

The light did no more than seep in, however, for the storm left in its wake gray, sullen skies and air that was warm and still. Frost went downstairs about six o'clock—Skippy had already learned to distinguish his lighter, hurried step from Devlin's heavy tread. Then, after a moment, he heard the man at the barn, and soon the low hum of the car was audible as he backed it out and around the house.

Silence reigned in the dismal place for another hour or so and then Skippy heard Devlin moving about in his room. When the man walked hurriedly downstairs, Nickie awoke, wild-eyed and staring.

"*Who—what's that?*" he whispered hoarsely.

"Just Devlin," Skippy answered. "What's the matter—you ain't been dreamin' like Timmy?"

Nickie ran his fingers through his straight black hair as he sat up. "I don't know—maybe so. I just get scared when I hear the least little sound in this joint. *Me*, that's never been scared of nothin'—hah!"

"I know," Skippy admitted. "I guess Devlin makes us feel that way, huh?"

Nickie nodded. "If I didn't hate the jug worse'n this house, I'd say, let's sneak."

"Maybe we'll have to," Skippy said softly, and nodded toward the sleeping Timmy. "If we stick round s'long as he's done an' get like he's now, I'd rather take a chance an' beat it."

Nickie nodded thoughtfully. "Anythin' you say, kid, an' I'm stringin' along. Even if you're only a kid, that bean of yours works all day."

Skippy warmed to Nickie for that tribute and he felt less afraid. It gave him a sense of strength to know that he had such an ally for he realized that he could do little alone.

Devlin called them gruffly to breakfast and the food wasn't bad. It would have been almost pleasant, Skippy ventured to remark, if they only had more light in the kitchen. Nickie agreed to this, but Timmy seemed in a daze.

After breakfast, Devlin made a concession which took them by surprise. "On account of the weather being so hot," he said gravely, "I'm going to let you boys stay outside a while."

"Gee!" Skippy murmured.

Devlin scowled. "It's taking a chance to let you out, but I'm counting on you not straying away from in sight of this house—*understand?*" After a pause, he added: "I got my reasons."

They understood only too well and made no further comment when Devlin unlocked the front door and sat on the ugly high stoop as they passed down and into the clearing about the house. Timmy sat on the bottom step, blinking his blue eyes and clasping and unclasping his hands.

"What's the matter?" Skippy asked sympathetically.

Timmy grinned. "I been in that dark house so long, my eyes don't know howta act, that's all." He took a long, deep breath of the murky air as if it were the utmost luxury. Then suddenly his thin, pale face became almost colorless and he nodded toward the right of the clearing. "Look!" he gasped.

The other boys turned and saw a huge evergreen tree spreading its branches over the sinister house. Not a breath of air rustled its broad boughs—it seemed to stand there waiting.

"The tree in my dream!" Timmy said, trembling. "I never seen it till now! When I come here it's night an' I don't notice it. I never looked out front—just now it's the first...."

"What's he talking about?" Devlin said, annoyed, from the top of the stoop.

"About that tree!" Nickie said, with ill-concealed contempt. "He had a terrible dream bout it last night—see?"

Devlin bit his lip and frowned. "It's nonsense! What's wrong with you, Timmy, eh?"

"What wouldn't be wrong, hah?" Nickie retorted sullenly. "If he'd stayed in the pen he wouldn't got no worse treatment than you give him—shuttin' him up a month in this hole till he's all shot. I ain't sayin' that it ain't better late than never, but even up in Delafield they don't keep a guy shut away from the daylight. Timmy or none of us *asked* you to spring us so you might give us a break an' treat us like human bein's."

Devlin's lips were set and grim and his beetle brows were so drawn that they made a deep furrow above his large nose. "Listen, you," he said angrily, "any more talk like that from you and you'll regret it. I'm running this and whether you did or didn't ask to be sprung, makes no difference. You'll keep your mouth shut—*understand!*"

The Greeks, smiling and silent until then, emitted a sound of dismay. Nickie mumbled something under his breath but made no other answer for the warning note in Devlin's voice was not to be misunderstood. Skippy gulped, and just then they heard the unmistakable sound of an old car chugging along through the narrow swamp trail.

Presently Frost appeared in the clearing, driving an ancient, dilapidated car that groaned and ground to a stop. The sight of it was amusing and the boys stared at it, smiling and curious. Timmy, however, did not share this curiosity.

He had taken one look at the car, and fainted.

CHAPTER XIV

TALK AMONG FRIENDS

The day dragged by and though Timmy seemed to have recovered from the effects of his spell, he moped around, melancholy and wrapped in his own gloomy thoughts.

"He's goin' nuts, that's what he is," Nickie whispered to Skippy after the evening meal was over.

"That's why we ain't stayin' to get like him," Skippy whispered back.

Nickie winked and nodded. He was beginning to see Skippy's point of view more and more.

They had cleared away the dishes and sat down to a game of cards at Shorty's suggestion, which was received with enthusiasm, and even Timmy had brightened and apparently put out of his mind the fears that had so unnerved him during the day.

Just before dusk, Devlin and Frost went out and locked the back door behind them. The boys hurried to the two back windows and peered out through the chinks in the shutters to watch the men go to the barn and presently back out in the queer looking car.

"Wonder where they're goin'?" Skippy asked of no one in particular.

"Oh, they'll be back," said Timmy grimly. "For *me!*" He lunged back to the table and took up his hand of cards with grim determination.

"Atta boy!" Skippy said. "Gee, Timmy, don't get down again, huh? Devlin can't *make* you do nothin' you don't wanta. You'll soon find out what he's gonna tell you to do. Beat it after that; soon's you get the chance."

"Yeah, some chance it'll be takin', I bet!" Timmy exclaimed. "I got a hunch an' that's all there's to it. But I ain't lettin' myself go off the handle no more—I wanta keep what nerve I got to tell Devlin where he's gettin' off if he springs any killin' jobs on *me.*"

"That goes double," Nickie said, suddenly very serious. "I don't like the look in Devlin's eye, he looks crazy b'lieve *me,* an' Timmy's right bout needin' all his nerve. He'll need it—we'll all need it when the time comes. An' lissen, guys, maybe we'll wanta know how we make out afterwards, hah? What d'ye say we dope out where we'll write letters to, hah?"

Shorty laughed. "Eet is funny, Neeckie. You talk lak that when mebbe we all see each other again some place out west together, eh? Ees that not what you thought when we come here, yes?"

"Yeah—I thought a lotta things when I come here," Nickie answered. "That's why I come. But I ain't so sure about Devlin sendin' us somewheres out west where we'll meet—see! He ain't said nothin', so I guess it means we say so long when we blow here. Anyways, we land some place; there ain't no sayin' there won't be somewheres we'll go, so I say let's write an' tell each other how we shook Devlin or how we didn't. Now I got a aunt where you guys can write me in New York. After I get fixed wherever I go, I'll tip her off an' she'll send me the letters."

"I got a aunt in Glens Falls," Timmy said brightening.

"I got a aunt in New York, too!" Skippy added. They all laughed at the coincidence, but Shorty and Biff broke into the conversation eagerly.

"I got Pop an' Mom in New York!" Shorty announced proudly.

"Me, too!" said Biff. "We leeve next door Shorty an' I bet they all crazy we don't show at Delafield."

They fell to talking about their parents proudly. Nickie did some reminiscing about his aunt's kindly care of him and it seemed that Timmy had somewhat the same story to tell. Skippy was listening intently, but at the same time his mind was going back to the night before when he had heard Devlin denouncing Frost for having brought the two Greeks along.

"Say, fellers," he said suddenly. "Shorty an' Biff got parents, huh? You, Nickie, an' Timmy an' me—we ain't got none. I heard Devlin an' Frost talkin' last night—I couldn't sleep so I heard what they said. One thing I know was that Devlin was burnin' up, 'cause he asked Frost what was he gonna do bout Shorty and Biff 'cause they're Greek'n' he couldn't pass 'em off for his sons. So Frost says he'll take 'em himself—one he'll take to Pittsburgh an' the other to Maine. Anyway, Devlin was mad that they came 'cause he said he didn't expect 'em. So you know what I think, fellers?"

"Spill it, kid," Nickie said.

"That Devlin picks on orphans a-purpose!"

"Say," Nickie said, admiringly, "that's brains, kid, an' I don't mean maybe. That's callin' the turn. Holy Smoke, if that don't seem like what he's doin'—the orphan racket, hah?" Nickie said as if to himself. "I wonder why, hah?"

Skippy grinned. "I doped out a little about him—maybe I can dope out the rest, huh?"

"Here's hopin', kid," Timmy said smiling. "Anyways, even if you don't, maybe when I find what's what an' get shipped west—maybe I can tip off the bulls so's you guys won't have no killin' jobs to do when Devlin puts the bee on you. It'd be better to go to Delafield an' get a couple years off on good behavior than be in the spot I'm in tonight."

"Yeah," said Nickie thoughtfully, "that's callin' the shot, Timmy. Even my full stretch'd be better'n what I'd get for goin' along with Devlin. Anyways, it ain't no bad idea to tip off the dicks if you can."

"You speak crazy!" Biff interrupted. "Timmy teep off, yes, but where he tell them deecks to find us, eh? Do we know where we are, eh?"

The looks they exchanged were an admission of defeat. After all, did Timmy know where he had been this past month and a half—did any of them in that damp, shadowy room have the slightest idea where the lonely house was situated? New York State? New Jersey? Pennsylvania? They might have been in the vast, trackless wilderness of Africa, so cleverly had Devlin concealed from them the location of that dismal house.

Skippy was reminded then of the boy Tucker about whom Mr. Conne had told him. Tucker hadn't known either where the house was located in which Devlin had kept him imprisoned for a full month. There was something very painstaking in Devlin's methods. He either completely confused his reform school "protégés" by taking them to live in a house and street which had its counterpart in hundreds of other houses and streets or else he confounded them utterly by driving them deep into this swampy wilderness under cover of night.

What were they to do?

An idea came to Skippy—why not write a letter and give it to Timmy to mail? In the next second, he was thankful that the impulse hadn't flourished under cold reasoning for he suddenly realized that Devlin would be just the man to anticipate that sort of thing and Timmy would be relieved of any such messages immediately. Also, he was reminded of Carlton Conne's warning: "Get in touch with no one, kid—tell no one *anything* unless you're certain that it's one of my men ... it's the only way that Dean Devlin can ever be caught ... and your job, kid, is to help me set the trap!"

His job—to help set the trap! What was he to do?

He was still asking himself that when Frost came into the back yard in the noisy, ancient car. Devlin had preceded him in the closed car and was already locking it up in the barn.

"Looks like they took the junk pile to get the big guy's closed car, hah?" Nickie said, not exactly at ease.

- 49 -

Timmy was looking over his shoulder, watching through the shutters the backyard scene under Devlin's powerful flashlight. "Looks like I'm gonna ride in the junk pile tonight," he said simply. "I wonder why, hey?"

Skippy felt suddenly choked and unable to utter a sound and, judging by the silence, the other boys were experiencing the same difficulty.

CHAPTER XV

HIS JOB

Even if they had been capable of speaking afterward, Devlin gave them little time. He came in, hurried upstairs and came down again in a few minutes, carrying a suitcase and wearing his usual dark clothes. He ordered Frost to stay close to the house until he returned. And without seeming to see the silent, staring boys he nodded at Timmy with some show of impatience.

"Time's short—come on!"

Skippy could still feel the strong, firm clasp of Timmy's handshake long after the ancient car clattered out of the back yard. He felt restless, and Nickie, that heroic defier of man-made petty laws, seemed stunned and fearful.

Shorty and Biff, a little too blunt to be long affected by anything, were comfortably seated again at the table arguing in their native tongue over a game of cards. Frost was seated opposite them, absorbed in a New York newspaper.

"All along I been sorta thinkin' we might be layin' it on kinda thick," Nickie whispered at Skippy's side. "Know what I mean? Aw, I thought mebbe we'd got thinkin' the worsta Devlin counta that funeral pan he's got an' the house an' all—see? People get jumpy just talkin' 'bout ghosts, don't they? Well, that's what I mean—I thought we got thinkin' he's a killer like Timmy done an' we couldn't thinka him as nothin' else. Up till just before they beat it I tells myself mebbe it's just his old racket, the swindlin' game that he's workin' in a new way with us kids as fall guys—see? But when I sees his face an' his eyes all funny an' starin' when he tells Timmy to c'mon, I get feelin' bad inside."

"Me too," Skippy agreed, after he had made certain that Frost was not watching them.

"Say, kid," Nickie said, between half-closed lips, "I ain't feelin' we're thinkin' the worsta him now. I'm feelin' that mebbe he's worse'n' what we think, he is—see!"

They sauntered toward the table at that juncture for Frost was looking up from his paper. His shrewd, colorless eyes observed them and his thin mouth was wrinkled mirthfully.

"Something in this here paper might give you kids a laff," he chuckled. "Here, sit down and read it—I gotta go up to my room and do a few things."

He was still chuckling when he left the kitchen but none of the boys paid him any attention then. They were too interested in the page which Nickie spread out and on which they read the headlines:

HOLD UP POLICE,

HELP BOYS FLEE

REFORMATORY TERM

Gangsters Wrest Four From Injured

Guards After Delafield Bound

Auto Is Ditched.

JOHN DOE IS RESCUED

He And Three Others Escape With

Armed Aid—Comb Country

For Fugitives.

There were two columns of the story. It had been discovered that the car had been tampered with and the driver told of being drawn into conversation while he was waiting at the courthouse by a "queer-looking man, dressed like a mechanic." Also, he described how the boys had been taken from him at the point of a gun and how Dippy Donovan had refused to escape. It was hinted at the reformatory that the boy, because of his behavior, stood a chance of having more than half his sentence remitted.

"They'd do that for us too, eh?" Shorty remarked regretfully. "The time eet go quick then an' when we got out we go 'ome, eh? Now we don't go 'ome teel we do stretch. Now we go west where Devlin send us. Always we are seeck for 'ome but we can't go."

"Yeah," said Nickie wistfully, "that's the trouble. It's justa bad break. I never give it a tumble before bout home, sweet home. All I thought was what a joke on them dicks when we pull a fast one. I never think how it ain't such a joke goin' west where we can't go home unless we take a rap. An' it'll be harder doin' the stretch afterward than now—why didn' I thinka that, hah?"

"I coulda told you if I hadn't been out," Skippy said thoughtfully.

"Yeah, sure thing, kid. You got brains. Me, I think I'm smart—see! I don't think how I'm gonna get homesick out west an' wanta see my aunt an' New York too. Holy Smoke, I don't wanna be dodgin' dicks forever!" he added, bitterly.

Bragging, laughing boy-heroes the day before, they were all bitter and resentful now. Their grand dream of escape, their defiance of the law, had brought them nothing but disappointment, and instead of knowing that each day brought them nearer to freedom, they were to be forever pursued by the spectral arm of the law. It threatened them with a double punishment should they come back voluntarily, yet it stood between them and their homes if they evaded it.

Skippy was absorbed in these thoughts just as if he had been one of them. He no longer felt that he was playing a part or acting as the spring of the trap into which Mr. Conne hoped Devlin would fall; he felt that the whole thing had become too realistic and that the spring of the trap was threatening to snap upon himself instead of Devlin.

Nickie broke into his musing. "Aw, we ain't gettin' nowheres by sittin' here mopin' about it, hah? C'mon, kid, let's play rummy."

Skippy had been turning the pages of the paper, giving them a cursory glance. As he turned to the ninth page he saw a column marked PERSONAL and directly under it he saw his name. His heart pounded furiously.

"Yeah, later," he said, trying to make his voice sound calm. "I gotta read the baseball news."

Nickie nodded absently for he was already absorbed in a good hand of cards which Biff had just dealt him. Skippy made certain that they were all equally absorbed; also, he made certain that Frost was still quiet upstairs. Then he proceeded to read.

SKIP: UNDERSTAND UNEXPECTED MOVE— SHOULD HAVE PREPARED FOR THAT ... YOU MUST SEND WORD SOMEHOW—IT'S YOUR JOB!... SIGNED "BOSS."

He must send word—*somehow! It was his job!* No one but Carlton Conne could have said it just like that—no one but Carlton Conne could have written it! And Skippy thrilled at the thought, thrilled each time he read the vivid message. He *would* get word to him somehow, particularly since he had seen in print that it was his job to do nothing else but! There was no doubt about it now.

Carlton Conne had signed himself as *Boss!*

CHAPTER XVI

A NOTE

A half hour later, Skippy had decided on one phase of his job. He climbed the dusty stairway and proceeded to the door of a room which no boy had been allowed to enter.

Frost answered his knock but did not ask him in. He had jumped up from a small, battered table upon which he had been writing, and now he stood in the open doorway, his colorless eyes searching Skippy's face in surprise.

"Can you lend me some paper an' pencil?" the boy asked briskly.

Frost's eyes narrowed. "What for?"

"To work out cross-word puzzles," Skippy answered, his eyes meeting Frost's gaze unflinchingly. "The kids are playin' cards an' I wanna do something." He laughed. "I work cross-word puzzles—every night!"

"Mm!" Frost seemed to be turning the thought over and over. Finally, he walked to the table and taking a bunch of keys from his pocket, he selected one and opened a little drawer. When he came back to the door he held out a pencil and two sheets of ordinary note-paper. "Here, kid," he said, chuckling, "cross-word puzzle all night if you feel like it."

Skippy took the paper smilingly but did not stop for further conversation. He wasn't taking any chances and he hurried downstairs again before Frost could think it over and perhaps recall him.

For an hour, Skippy scribbled and wrote all over one sheet of the paper. The other piece of paper along with a pencil of his own he carefully concealed under his belt. And, when the game of rummy was broken up around midnight, the boy had torn his scribbling sheet into a hundred bits and scattered it on the table. Then when they went upstairs, he returned the pencil to Frost.

Fifteen minutes later, he saw the rim of light disappear from under the door jamb and he knew that Frost had blown out his lantern and was going to bed. He waited breathlessly then and after some minutes got out of bed and tiptoed to the door where he listened intently.

It was some time before he was rewarded with the sound of Frost's first labored snore. Then he roused Fallon.

"Don't make a sound, Nick," he whispered.

"I won't, kid!" Nickie murmured sleepily. Then he sat up. "What's wrong?"

"I'm gonna write a note, Nickie—I'll tell you why after. What I want you to do is go over to the door an' listen for Frost's snore. If he stops, gimme the high sign. I'm gonna light the lantern an' take it over by the window. The light won't show into the hall from there."

"Good dope, kid," Nickie agreed, stepping out onto the floor. "But what you gonna write with, hah? You gave Frost back the pencil."

Skippy winked. "I got my own, but I didn't wanna make him suspicious. I wanted some paper so's I could write this note tonight when I got the chance. If I didn't ask for a pencil, then he'd know I had one—get me? I tore up the one sheet I scribbled on—tore it up in a lotta pieces so's he could see it. He won't know whether it's one or two sheets of his paper that I used an' I'm takin' a chance he thinks it's the two sheets. Anyway, I don't think he'll give it a thought that I held back the other sheet 'cause I give him back the pencil."

"Kid, there's no mud on you," said Nickie admiringly. "Get the lantern an' write your note. I'll listen an' if I hear a peep outa him, I'll cough—see?"

Skippy got the lantern down from the hook on the side wall. He took it over to the window and set it down firmly on the sill, then spread out the neatly folded note-paper and began to write:

"After the accident we rode and rode—through woods and every place, I don't know where. It was eight or nine o'clock when we got here, a terrible lonesome house with swamp and woods all round. It's got bars all inside on the windows so we can't get out. A boy named Timmy Brogan went with him tonight so a feller named Frost (his pal) is here with us now. There's three kids besides me and maybe by the time you get this two will be gone. Anyway, boss, all I can tell you about it, is Frost said this house used to be in a village but the village burned down all round it. So instead of building up the village again the people moved twenty-five miles away near a railroad—that was seventy-five years ago. Frost says it's the house that people forgot and he says nobody knew about it but a nit-wit hermit that died last year. So this is all I know about where I am. I get headaches kind of from it being so hot in this house with all the shutters closed too, but outside of that, I'm all right. Devlin's terrible mysterious and queer acting boss and the kid that went tonight said *he* was a worse man than ever you think. Anyway, I hope I can give this to somebody soon so you can find out where we are and help us.... Skip"....

Nickie was still a patient sentinel and he smiled encouragingly. Skippy took heart and folded up the note and wrote outside:

"To Whoever Gets this Will they Please send this to the Manhattan World, New York City ... thanks.... And keep this a secret or else we'll be taken away and won't get helped!"

Below it, he added:

"To the Editor of the Personal Column.... An Answer to Boss' in Friday's paper, August 19...."

He put down his pencil and folded the note still smaller. Then he got one of his shoes and slipped the paper inside of the loose lining. After that, he nodded to Nickie and putting the light out they crawled into bed.

"Devlin'll be takin' one of us to go through that doctor's examination business soon's he gets back, Nickie," Skippy whispered. "Whoever he takes, will take that note 'cause it'll bring us help if we wait our chance an' slip it to somebody we think we can trust. We'll pass somebody going back an' forth to the doctor's office an' it's better if it's a lady."

"Yeah, an *old* lady," Nickie murmured, thinking wistfully of his good aunt. "Them you can trust."

"For two reasons we shouldn't give it to the doctor," Skippy warned. "Devlin might get wise, an' besides the doctor might be workin' with Devlin. So we gotta be careful, huh?"

"You tell 'em! Kid, you're a wonder at dopin' out things. If it wasn't for you, I'd be in the dumps—you keep a guy all pepped up."

"Aw, it ain't anything. I wanna help myself too, don't I? But I trust you, Nickie, honest. I wouldn't let you in on this if I didn't. Shorty and Biff are out 'cause I don't feel sure of 'em."

"Yeah, they're too dumb. But take it from me—Nickie Fallon's been your pal from the minute I saw you—see? An' that means it's all jake between us. Justa show how much you can trust me, kid, I won't even read that note if I'm gonna be the one to take it. I'll keep it in my shoe till Devlin ain't lookin' an' I see that old lady. What you wrote's your business an' I ain't buttin' in."

Skippy knew that Fallon was sincere. And though, at first, he was a little fearful that he had not obeyed orders strictly to the letter, he knew that Carlton Conne would understand that he *had* to take Nickie into his confidence this little bit. He had purposely refrained from sending the message direct to the great detective or bringing the name of the

International Detective Agency into it in any way lest the note should fall into unfriendly hands.

After all, he told himself, no one, not even Nickie, could guess who he was or the part he was playing, from the contents of that note. Certainly, Devlin wouldn't guess, if he read it, that the man addressed as "Boss" was the man who was determined to track him down—none other than that famous detective, Carlton Conne!

He had done all that he could do now. They had to be patient and wait until one or the other could safely place the note in the hands of some trustworthy person. Thus far they were safe and sound, Skippy assured himself. At least they were tonight.

But what of tomorrow?

CHAPTER XVII

A CHANGE OF PLANS

The day dawned cloudy and gray and when Skippy woke at eight o'clock he looked in vain for a ray of heartening sunlight. Nothing but warm air came in through the shutters and it was sticky and close.

Nickie sat up and stretched lazily. "Wow! What a headache, kid," he said, rubbing his forehead. "How's yours, hah?"

"Bad as last night," Skippy answered mournfully. "We gotta expect headaches in a hot, dark house like this, huh? Gee whiz, Nickie, sump'n's gotta happen to get us outa here soon or I'll be like Timmy, I guess. Here it's only the second mornin' an' I feel like it's a year."

Nickie was up and listening at the door while Skippy was talking. "Where is he?" he asked, on the alert.

"Frost went downstairs most an hour ago, so don't worry. I heard him walkin' an' walkin' round his room just like he had sump'n on his mind. Then all of a sudden he comes out into the hall 'n' locks his door like he always does an' beats it downstairs. Sump'n must be up."

Skippy was right—something was up. They found out what it was when they appeared in the kitchen for breakfast a few minutes later. Frost was hurrying back and forth from the yard and down to the cellar bearing pails of water from the pump outside.

"I'm putting five days' water supply in the crock down cellar," he explained after his last trip. "Keep the cover on it tight like I'm leaving it, and it'll stay fresh and cold. There's canned stuff and other grub so you can feed and I'll show you how else you can manage before I leave."

"You beatin' it?" Nickie asked.

"Mm," Frost murmured. His colorless eyes dropped before their gaze. And, as if to change the subject, he asked: "D'ye know if them Greek kids are awake?"

"No, we didn't hear a thing when we come down," Skippy answered promptly. Then, out of a clear sky he hurled the query: "Why, you ain't takin' 'em away, are you, Mr. Frost?"

Frost was disconcerted. "Why—er—sure!" he stammered. "I am! I—if Dev—if Barker comes back—he should be here by Wednesday, tell him there's a note in the room explainin' matters." He blinked his colorless eyes, then added: "I'm lockin' you kids up for five days, but I'm leavin' you the run of the house—that's how much I trust you!"

"Says you!" Nickie sneered.

Points of color appeared upon Frost's cheeks. He glared at Fallon and asked, "What d'ye mean, hey?"

"Ain't them ears pinned on your head?" was Nickie's retort. "It looks like we're trusted with bars all over the joint an' even on the cellar winders, hah? It looks like we're trusted when the bars ain't even enough, so you hadda padlock all the shutters too. Yeah, that stuff goes for Sweeny."

"That's Dev—Barker's idea—not mine—get me? Anyway, I ain't got no time to argue. We'll hash it over when I get back," Frost snapped.

He turned, went upstairs and Nickie proceeded with the making of coffee. Skippy got a package of bacon from the cupboard and silently set about the task of frying it. Words wouldn't come—he could do nothing but listen and wait. For what, he didn't know.

When Shorty and Biff came downstairs and back to the kitchen they were their usual smiling selves. Nickie looked from his coffee pot to them and Skippy's eyes traveled back and forth from their round faces to the briskly frying bacon.

"Frost tell you he's beatin' it with you guys this morning?" Nickie asked.

"Sure," Biff smiled.

"And you ain't nervous or nothin', hah?" Nickie asked, amazed that Biff could smile.

"Nah. The queecker we go, the queecker comes the time we sneak home."

"We theenk maybe we tell dees Frost we rather not go to Peetsburgh or Maine or what it ees he wants to take us," Shorty spoke up. "We theenk we ask heem to take us home so we can say hello, then we go Delafield. Maybe they lop off time for us too 'cause we come back, eh?"

"Maybe," Skippy said in a small voice.

"You never can tell," Nickie said, his eyes staring into space.

They ate in silence, a strange oppressive silence, and Skippy felt almost glad when Frost's hurried steps sounded on the stairs. If it had to be, it was better to have it over now than to endure the tension of waiting and living in dread.

A smile and a handclasp and they were gone. Nickie and Skippy stood listening as Frost locked the woodshed door from the outside. When the car chugged softly outside they made no attempt to go to the windows and look. Neither one moved an inch until the sound of the motor had ceased to echo in the clearing.

"If I thought Frost didn't have no gun, I'd jumped him," said Nickie at last. "But catch him and Devlin in a racket like this without carryin' rods, hah?"

Skippy was again reminded of Carlton Conne's assurance that Dean Devlin was not the gun-toting kind of criminal. The boy had no doubt but that that had been true of Devlin once, but not now. Too, the detective had said that Devlin was after people's money—not people. In the light of what Skippy now knew, that also was no longer true. Devlin had evidently made rapid strides in criminality. He had taken on a partner and whatever his mystery racket was, the fact that he trafficked in these convicted boys, evidently for gain, robbed him completely of the superficial glamour his adventurous life might have previously given him.

"Say, Nickie," Skippy said at length, "we got five days here alone an' if we can't do a Houdini in that time we're a coupla bums."

Nickie's face became radiant. "Gotta plan, kid?"

"I gotta hunch maybe we can work loose a coupla bars in some window! If we can't find a crowbar, maybe we'll find sump'n else, huh? We'll start down cellar right away."

"You said it, kid!" Nickie was enthusiastic. "And when we scram outa this drum, I'll say like Biff and Shorty, we'll go home'n' say hello an' then tell the dicks we're reportin' for Delafield."

Skippy thought of an old saying of his aunt's about an ill wind blowing someone some good. Timmy, the Greeks, and now Nickie all seemed to lose their defiance of the law under Devlin's evil roof. If it took an evil to cure an evil then their contact with the arch criminal had not been entirely in vain.

CHAPTER XVIII

THE SEARCH

The cellar yielded nothing in their search but mouldy rubbish, ancient cobwebs and the stone crock which Frost had indicated as their water supply. A broken shovel which Skippy salvaged from one of the rubbish piles was dragged upstairs with the forlorn hope that it might prove useful if they found nothing better.

The kitchen cupboard was next attacked but after an hour's work they found that that too availed them nothing. Warm and perspiring, they walked through the gloomy rooms and sat down to rest in the vast, almost dark parlor. Skippy looked around at the chairs and sighed.

"We've gotta find sump'n, Nickie!" he said. "It ain't gonna be no joke sittin' here an' knowin' we *could* get out if we had sump'n to work with!"

"Don't I know it, kid!" Nickie said, running his fingers through his straight, black hair. "It's like night all the time in here an' the empty rooms an' creakin' floors'd drive anybody nuts." Suddenly he straightened up, tense with a new idea. "Lissen, kid! How bout their room, hah? They'd be wise that we'd go huntin' sump'n, so what they don't want us findin' they lock in their room, hah? That's it—*their room*!"

"Yeah, but it's locked," Skippy reminded him.

"Sure, it's locked," Nickie admitted smilingly. "But that's where I come in—see? Whadda you s'pose the dicks grabbed me for, hah? Listen, there ain't no lock I can't pick if I stick at it long enough. I'd pick them doors downstairs if they wasn't metal an' outside locks."

Skippy could not conceal his smile.

Nickie grinned too. "Aw, don't worry, kid. It'll be the last lock I ever pick." Suddenly he was serious and looked straight at Skippy. "Say, kid, I can't believe you ever beat the law even onct."

"Nope."

"Holy Smoke! Framed, hah?"

"Sorta."

"If I could lay my mitts on the guy what...."

"Aw, forget it, Nickie," Skippy said, rising. "When we get away we'll talk about it, huh? Gee whiz, I'm here an' so we gotta be thinkin' bout gettin' out quick's we can."

They went hopefully upstairs. Armed with a small kitchen knife Nickie started operations at the keyhole of the room which Frost and Devlin occupied but it was late that afternoon when it yielded.

They burst into this private and mysterious sanctum with cries of joy, then stopped a little beyond the threshold and surveyed the room with a feeling of disappointment. It was furnished little better than their room and aside from an old iron bed, there was a single chair, a trunk, and a cracked mirror which hung over the dilapidated writing table.

There were two windows, barred and shuttered like the rest of the house. Skippy noticed that, then walked to the far end of the room and opened a closet door.

"A ladder, Nickie!" he exclaimed, joyfully. "I betcha it's a ladder for the attic!"

"Yeah, an' what we gonna do up in the attic, hah, kid?" Nickie asked. "Even if there wasn't no bars to them winders up there, what'd we do, hah?"

"Did I say I knew what we'd do? Ain't it sump'n that we found sump'n? Gee whiz, it's sump'n that the ladder gets us *somewheres*, even if it's the attic where we can't do anything."

Nickie's keen, smiling eyes had already found something of interest on the writing table. "A note to the big cheese, kid. From Frost. It's short and sweet. C'mon, take a look."

Skippy picked up the paper and read: "I got a great scheme early this morning, boss, so I'm taking the Greeks to Pittsburgh—get me? I thought no use hanging round here till you got back ... I could have things moving, maybe even over by that time. I won't hog the price on account of what you said but I thought I can kill two birds with one stone. I can have two Greek sons as well as one, can't I? Now, I'm going so I'll see you when I get back...." It was unsigned.

Nickie looked disappointed. "Still we don't know what their racket is, hah? There's a price an' I wonder what for? S'help me, kid, I'm stumped."

"Me too," Skippy admitted, opening the table drawer curiously and peering inside. He drew out a small memorandum book and opened it. Suddenly he whistled. "If you wanna know what the price's for, this'll tell us, Nickie. Gee whiz, here's prices *an' how*! He's got a price for us."

"You're crazy!" Nickie said. "A price for us?"

He soon saw with his own eyes that Devlin had listed boys, prices, dates and places over a period of several months. Also, it was quite evident that there had been little variation in the means by which they came into the man's dubious protection. Against Timmy Brogan's name was listed a price of $2,500. At the top of a page, underlined in red, was the name of Tucker, who seemed to have been a $3,000 loss to Devlin.

Turning the next page, which bore a date two days old, the boys looked at their own names. Nickie was rated at $3,000 and Skippy at $2,500. Shorty and Biff were question-marked at $1,000, and in parentheses the probable price of $500 each was printed.

"At three grand I'm the most expensive guy in the bunch," Nickie laughed nervously. "How you make it out?"

Skippy shrugged. "You're askin' me! What's all these prices for us anyway, huh? Why do they all go from $500 to $3,000—what could it be for? Gee whiz, Nickie, we ain't gettin' anywheres with this."

"Don't I know it, kid? We should worry about what we don't know. Let's look through the trunk an' the closet an' if that ain't no help, we'll go up in the attic an' chase rats."

Skippy laughed. "An' how!" he said. "If we can't get out we can give the rats a break anyway, huh? Devlin might put a price on 'em if he comes back an' finds 'em here."

Without any definite motive, Skippy walked over to the back window and looked out through a good-sized chink in the shutters where two of the slats had fallen out. A rain barrel stood just beneath the window, and on the surface of the water a green slime had gathered, an excellent playground for mosquitoes.

He watched it for a moment, then with a sudden idea, he let the notebook slip from his hands and saw it slide down the side of the building and out of sight behind the rain-barrel.

"Say, you gone nuts?" Nickie exclaimed.

"I don't know," Skippy answered honestly. "I'm playin' a hunch—don't ask me why! It was like—aw, you know what I mean, Nickie—like Fate!"

It *was* Fate—Skippy was to realize that before another twenty-four hours had passed.

CHAPTER XIX

HOPE IN THE ATTIC

Shadows of early evening were beginning to creep over the silent swamp land before the boys hit upon a practicable plan of escape. They had had two hours' hunt through the dust-choked attic, braving a seventy-five year accumulation of rubbish which generations of rats had chewed and scattered to its four corners.

They found a trunk of ancient vintage that still held up sufficiently to enable them to sit down and rest upon it. Before them, the front attic window offered possibilities and they were discussing it pro and con. Also, they had been able to open it and because it lacked shutters they enjoyed what was left of the daylight and welcomed the occasional damp, warm breeze that blew in.

Skippy had found in the rubbish a coil of rope that was in excellent condition. Nickie had come upon what apparently had been the handle of an antique iron pot, and the two discoveries had formed the nucleus of their present discussion.

The giant evergreen of poor Timmy's dream spread its lofty boughs within a few yards of the small window. "That pot handle's strong enough to wedge out those bars, Nickie," Skippy was saying thoughtfully. "It'll take maybe a coupla hours, 'cause I guess they're in there pretty tight. When we get that done, I'll lasso that tree an' tie it pretty tight somewheres in here."

"I getcha, kid!" Nickie said enthusiastically. "We swing out along it hand over hand, hah? Then, when we hit a strong-lookin' branch we drop an' zip, we're on the ground fore we know it!"

"Yeah, that's it. It's the only way. We been all over this house an' this is the best we can do."

"Sure. It's work but ain't it worth it? Anyways, kid, let's put the bag on. We ain't had no chow all day, we been so busy turnin' this place upside down. How about it?"

"Gee whiz, I most forgot I had a stomach—honest! I can't thinka nothin' but gettin' away. But I'm hungry, that's a fact."

"Yeah, me too. Even them canned beans'll taste like turkey tonight."

"*Beans!*" Skippy said disgustedly. "It'll be nice to eat sump'n besides canned beans n' stale crackers n' coffee. Gee whiz, I like milk, I do—cold, creamy milk!"

"Yeah, an' I like soup, kid. Nice, hot, creamy soup like my aunt makes."

"C'mon, Nickie, let's get eatin' an' get it over with!"

Just as they descended the ladder they heard, far in the east, a low rumble of thunder. Before they had started to feast on their beans, there was no doubt that a storm was fast approaching. The wind was rising steadily and the swaying trees made eerie sounds which they could plainly hear during frequent lapses of conversation.

"Hope it ain't gonna be like the other night," Skippy said earnestly. "The room was hot but I shivered just the same. An' then Timmy havin' that dream an' screamin' like he did...."

"Yeah, I was glad I was asleep. Outside this graveyard, there ain't nothin' gives me the jitters worse'n a bad storm. Holy Smoke, I ain't myself then."

There was a terrific clap of thunder and the wind screeched mockingly past the kitchen windows. A shutter somewhere on the house creaked uneasily on its rusted hinges. The boys put down their coffee cups and looked at each other.

"Takes a hard storm like this for clearin' the air," said Nickie profoundly. "My aunt always says that. Remember since the other night it's been so gloomy—ain't even seen no sun since we been here. Maybe it'll be clear tomorrer."

"Yeah, maybe."

"Anyways, kid, will we beat it right off if we get them bars loose tonight?"

"Sure, if we get 'em loose. But it ain't gonna be so easy, Nickie."

And it wasn't easy—not at all. They took turns at the top bar and after an hour succeeded in making it yield only a little and on one side at that. The lantern light was feeble and they dared not use two lamps at a time, for they had made the discovery before climbing to the attic that the oil supply which Frost had left them was too low to be used freely.

The wind screamed around under the eaves and presently blew the rain through the open window. Vainly, they tried to close it but having been in disuse for so many years the frame had warped and Skippy soon decided that it would take a chisel and hammer to get results.

"How about them newspapers in the cellar, kid?" Nickie suggested. "We can pin 'em up against there while we work."

"Pin 'em with what? Gee whiz, use your bean."

"Yeah, you're right, kid. We gotta get wet an' like it."

"Not if you wanna quit till tomorrow. An' I don't like to do that, Nickie. Sump'n tells me do what we can tonight."

"Just's you say, kid. I'm gettin' so's I feel you're a reg'lar mascot—see? I ain't doin' nothin' without you sayin' it's K. O."

Skippy grinned and took his turn at the window. The thunder was rolling away into the distance but the heat lightning blazed across the black sky at frequent intervals. The moaning wind echoed back and forth mournfully and the rain made a hissing noise as it lashed the window sill.

Fallon had pulled the trunk as near the window as possible. He made a doleful picture sitting there, the lantern held at arm's length so as to give Skippy light. His pale face was in a half-shadow and his narrow shoulders drooped dejectedly. Suddenly he looked up and his black eyes were questioning.

"Hear a noise, kid?"

Skippy stopped his tugging at the top bar and shook his head. "What kinda noise?"

"Like somebuddy runnin'. Maybe I'm crazy—just hearin' things."

"The wind an' the rain, I betcha," Skippy said, getting back to his task. "It'll last all night—I think it's gettin' cooler."

"Yeah, an' you'n me's gettin' wetter. We'll be plenty cool by the time we get through. Gimme a whack at it now, hah?"

"Wait a minute. I ain't tired yet—it's loosened a little more."

Nickie sighed. "Just on one side yet, hah? Holy smoke, at that speed...." Then, suddenly: "Kid, I hear somebuddy! Somebuddy runnin'!"

Before Skippy could answer they were startled by a cry that seemed to come from the clearing.

"HE JUST STOOD WAITIN' FOR ME TO DROWN!"

CHAPTER XX

TIMMY?

Nickie jumped up and held the lantern high over their heads. They looked down into the clearing but for a long time the black night and the screaming wind and rain obscured their vision. Skippy thought he saw something moving but he wasn't sure.

Again a thin, piteous scream pierced the storm. *Nickie—Kid? Can't you guys hear me? It's me—Timmy!*"

"*Timmy!*" Skippy shouted. "What...."

"Listen," came the cry, "I wanta tell you guys ... that's why I come back ... I'm hurt—I don't know how I found this place, honest! Somethin' made my feet run this way so's I could tell you ... he's got no heart ... he's...."

"We'll come down, Timmy—in front!" Skippy shouted. "Downstairs!"

"It won't do no good!" came the answer. "You can't get out unless he leaves you—then beat it for your life!" There was a pause, then: "Frost ... where's he?"

"He ain't here, Timmy!" Nickie cried, finding his voice. He swung the lantern higher and then, for the first time, they could see the slight form swaying down by the evergreen tree.

"I just come back to tell you." Timmy's voice was a heart-rending sob. "He's what I told you ... it's a trick! He makes out somethin's wrong with the car an' he makes me get behind the wheel n' tells me to step on the gas an' come toward him. It's dark an' I see him standing there up the road.... I don't know ... when I get most to him he jumps an' it's a bridge.... I go right over in the car!" He groaned audibly.

"We gotta get out an' help you, Timmy!" Skippy cried.

"I'm goin' right away—you can't get out, you know you can't!" After a pause, he cried: "Listen, it wasn't no accident—I hit my head on the way down an' in the water when I come up I yelled an' I knew he was standin' up on the bridge ... he wouldn't help me ... he just stood waitin' for me to drown I But I didn't ... I grabbed a log an' pushed myself up an' he didn't see me climb up...."

"Where's *he*?" Nickie called nervously.

"He was up there—on the bridge—when I sneaked away through the trees ... he acted like he was waitin' for a car to come along. I didn't meet any ... anyhow, all I could think of was to come here an' tip you off.... I was sick.... I slep' in the woods all day and ... I knew he wouldn' be here—I knew he'd be lookin' in the lake for me.... *Listen!*"

The lantern swayed in Nickie's trembling hand. The light flickered and sputtered with each fresh onslaught of the wind. Skippy held the top bar and pressed his face into the opening, his heart beating like a triphammer. There was a sound in the distance and the fear of what it might be caused him to gulp with dismay.

"*It's a car!*" Timmy screamed. "A car!"

"What'd you come for, Timmy?" Nickie shouted frantically.

"*Run! Hide!*" Skippy was crying.

Timmy's slim form seemed to be swaying uncertainly. He took a few steps nearer the great tree, acting as if he were bewildered.

Skippy no longer heard the sound and said so. Nickie agreed with him. They cried down to Timmy to hurry—to run, but the boy looked up at them vaguely and shrugged his shoulders mechanically.

"He's too sick—too hurt!" Skippy cried, pulling at Nickie's sleeve. "He don't seem to move, he can't!"

The lantern seemed to be making a desperate effort to light up the scene. Its rays struggled high over Nickie's head and shone down almost brightly for a precious moment, down upon Timmy's upturned face.

He was smiling ... or did they imagine it? His regular features slowly froze—froze into a horrified expression ... or were they imagining that too? And that arm that stole out from behind the great evergreen.... Suddenly, there was a muffled scream, a voice that sounded like Timmy's.

Then the lantern light went out, leaving them in darkness.

CHAPTER XXI

DO DREAMS COME TRUE?

Nickie was clinging to him and making funny little noises deep in his throat. Skippy let him cling, for he was shaking from head to foot himself and he blinked his eyes in the darkness.

"You seen *him*—you seen—" Skippy stammered, frightened at the sound of his own voice.

"I don't know what I seen," Nickie said, his words scarcely audible because of his chattering teeth. "I—that scream—you heard that, hah?"

"Sure, and I seen him look terrible. Lissen!" Mechanically, they put out their hands to feel for the window and pressed close to it oblivious of the fresh downpour of rain which swept in upon them, drenching them to the skin. The gale screamed its hardest, the lantern creaked in Nickie's shaking hand like some spectral voice out of the night, but that was the only sound to reach their listening ears.

"*Timmy!*" Skippy called suddenly. "Timmy—*answer!*"

"You hurt, Timmy?" Nickie's query was pathetic.

A tense silence seemed to beat upon their ears and for a while they had difficulty in even listening to the noises of the storm. Their eagerness to hear Timmy's thin voice had plunged them into a temporary oblivion from which they recovered with a start.

"You believe in spooks?" Nickie asked in a whisper.

"Nope." Skippy gulped. "Why?"

"Call once again, hah?"

Skippy called, loud and long.

The wind screamed in answer, mockingly.

"Let's beat it downstairs an' have some light, hah?" After a pause: "You ain't got matches, I s'pose?"

"Would I be standin' here in the dark?"

Nickie's throat was full of noises. "We better be careful goin' down the ladder—say, we didn't leave the lantern in the hall lighted."

"An' the one in the kitchen too," Skippy reminded him grimly. "There ain't no light till we get to the kitchen n' find a match."

Nickie stopped short. "Where's that rope an' that iron handle?" he asked fearfully.

"I hid 'em under that rubbish by the window just now. So go on. Le's get down."

Nickie sighed. "I oughta knowed you wouldn't forget nothin' even at a time like this."

They groped their way down the ladder and waited for a moment in the upper hall listening to the various sounds throughout the house and the noise of the storm. They could not see each other and they instinctively pressed their bodies close together. Nickie had his hand through Skippy's arm and clung to it tightly. Then by a mutual impulse they moved toward the stairway with measured steps, their ears strained and listening for all that their eyes could not see.

It was a long and awesome journey to the bottom of the stairway and once there they had a whispered consultation as to whether to go around through the rooms to the kitchen or march straight past the cellar door and so on into the room. Skippy decided on keeping to the hall even though it meant passing the door to the dim regions below.

They had not taken two steps in that direction, when Nickie gave vent to a blood-curdling scream.

"*What?*" Skippy cried frantically.

"*My foot!*" Nickie was gasping in the dark. "Sump'n run over my foot!"

"*A rat!*" Skippy said, disgustedly. "I said to shut that cellar door, Nickie!"

"Oh my head!" Nickie groaned. "I was scared skinny. Kid, let's run."

Skippy was human enough to accede and they made the kitchen in one breath-taking bound.

Nickie let go his hold on the other's arm. "Whew!" he said nervously. "Gimme a match."

"Yeah, that's what I say," Skippy said, moving noisily about the room. "They ain't on this stove—I've felt all over. Say, you lit that lantern we took up to the attic."

"Sure, I did. Wha'd I do with them matches?" Nickie asked himself desperately.

It was another day before he found out, and in the interim they had decided that there was no other room in the house which offered the comparative peace of their own room. At least they could shut themselves in there. And that they did, not stopping until they had pushed their heavy bed tight against the stout oaken door.

"What we afraid of, huh?" Skippy asked in a small voice. They had undressed and were in bed.

"I dunno, kid!" Nickie admitted honestly. "I'm kinda broke up in a hundred pieces like, since that scream."

"*Timmy's?*"

"Say, was it sure enough him?"

"Why, sure—gee whiz, who else...."

"That's why I ast if you believe'n spooks!"

"Nickie! Gee whiz, we heard Timmy talkin'—didn't he tell us twas all a trick with Devlin—didn't he say Devlin meant to kill him and...."

"Yeah, an' ain't that like his dream the other night? Ain't it like he comes back in his dream an' stands under that big tree? Ain't it all in his dream how he's tellin' us up at the winder an' warnin' us, when zip, he sees this arm come out an' pretty soon he feels like he's chokin'? How do we know he ain't kicked off somehow last night an' tonight he comes back from the dead, hah?"

Frightened as he was, Skippy could not help smiling into the darkness. "Say, I thought you was a real tough guy when I first spotted you. An' here you're talkin' bout spooks an' comin' back from the dead like you're a regular sissy."

Nickie did not protest. Something had happened to him and he was incapable of explaining just what it was. The tough guy, as Skippy termed it, no longer existed, for Nickie had looked upon an evil which had shaken him to his very soul. He did not know it then, but the small sins which were directly responsible for his present predicament had gone, never to return.

"I dunno, kid," he said, slowly, "but it's like I'm payin' for doin' what I done an' makin' my aunt cry an' worry after she brought me up. I knowed it worried her but I kep' on stubborn-like so now I got it good! Long's I live I won't never forget Timmy's scream, whether it was him'r his spook!"

"Maybe it was good then that this happened," Skippy said practically. "Whether it was Timmy's ghost or not." But after a pause, he added, fearfully: "Gee whiz, Timmy *can't* be dead!"

"I think different, kid. I think he is!"

"But we heard him talk, Nickie. You an' me, we heard it like we hear each other talkin' now, didn't we?"

"Sure. But ain't it funny, kid, how it's all like it was in that dream he told us about?"

"I'll say it's funny. It's like his dream so much that it gives me the creeps. Even to the part where he told us how he stood by the evergreen tree an' then sudden like when he's warnin' us to beat it, them arms reached out n' grabbed him an' he felt like he was chokin' to death. Gee whiz! If the two of us didn't hear him speak, I'd say there was sump'n spooky about it. We even heard the car!"

"Sure, we did. An' we see somethin' dark like a guy's arms reach out from behind that tree, didn't we?"

"I couldn't swear I did, Nickie. It chokes me when I think of it. Lissen, you don't think that was really Devlin—that he could really ki—kill Timmy?"

"Kid, since I been here, I don't know what's real an' what ain't—see? All I know is I'll go nutty if there's any more goin's on like we see tonight."

Skippy was of the same mind, but he didn't say so. He would have given much to know just how much was imagination and how much was stark reality. Timmy's empty cot, a vague shadow against the side wall, did much to keep these dreadful thoughts in his mind. Through wearying hours the scream of his dreams and his scream in the clearing seemed to echo mockingly through the storm. Skippy felt exhausted, yet all through the long night the question revolved in his mind.

Was it a dream come true?

CHAPTER XXII

DEVLIN'S RETURN

Nickie slept after a long time but Skippy was not so fortunate. Not until the storm settled down into a steady pattering rain with the early morning hours did he find himself dozing, yet always waking suddenly, trembling, and with his heart beating rapidly in his breast.

During one of these quiet intervals in which he was dozing, he thought he dreamed that he heard the sound of a car. He did not wake at once, but kept listening for it again in a more or less semi-conscious state. Suddenly, however, he was sure that he heard footsteps down in the kitchen.

For a moment he felt frozen with terror. Then he gathered himself together and shook Nickie firmly. "Don't speak, Nickie!" he whispered. "Just *lissen!*"

Nickie was wide awake and alert, but he did not move a muscle. "I hear it, kid," he murmured. "Somebuddy in the kitchen."

"Yep. I'm frozen like."

"Me too. What'll we do, hah?"

"Stay where we are when we ain't got a light."

"Right. I forgot. Who d'you think tis?"

"*Lissen!*"

They listened intently. A muffled cough, the sound of something metallic falling, nothing escaped them. The footsteps were measured and heavy and seemed to circle the kitchen interminably.

"Sounds like *him*, kid!" Nickie whispered fearfully. "I know them big feeta his'n. He's got the biggest dogs I ever seen. Ever notice?"

"Nope." Skippy thought how queer that Nickie should speak of such details at a fearful time like this. But people did that—he was beginning to realize that one was apt to say and do almost anything strange in moments of distress.

"Say, kid!"

"Yeah?"

"If it's *him* ... what bout that lock I picked in his room ... what about the ladder?"

- 74 -

"I been thinkin'," Skippy answered breathlessly. "Lissen, Nick—you don't know nothin' bout that lock, neither do I! Frost said sump'n about how he lost his keys when he was beatin' it with Shorty and Biff—get me? He musta picked the lock himself. We found the door that way when we come upstairs after they blew. We were lookin' for a ladder to go up in the attic—we wanted to go up an' snoop round for sump'n to do. We seen the closet door standin' open an' there was the ladder."

"Oke, kid. But s'pose he's leary bout us wantin' to go up in the attic?"

"I gotta hunch he won't be—much. We didn't wedge the bar enough so's he'd notice it less he went up an' looked close. Even then he'd know it'd be too far to jump out the winder an' he won't get wise bout the tree less he sees the rope. Gee whiz, I'm glad I hid it, I am."

"I could cry, I'm so glad, kid. This racket's too spooky for me to think up an alibi quick. Holy smoke, you're a life-saver!"

At heart, Skippy felt no such assurance. He was shaking from head to foot and he dreaded Devlin as he dreaded Death. He shuddered at the unconscious simile and wondered if the very thought itself did not portend the evil which Timmy had come back to warn them of.

Nickie's cold, clammy hand stole over and grasped his trembling wrist. Unashamed, they interlaced their fingers and clasped them so firmly that it hurt. Nevertheless, they derived a sort of comfort from the contact and breathed more freely even after the heavy feet below tramped out of the kitchen and they heard the measured tread into the hall.

"He's comin', I bet!" Skippy whispered feverishly.

Nickie was mumbling a prayer that his aunt had taught him in babyhood, a prayer that he thought he had forgotten long ago. He dared not speak, nor think, for fear of screaming and acting like a weak, hysterical girl. The prayer and Skippy's warm fingers pressing against his own kept him from losing his head entirely.

Then they heard the footsteps on the stair!

Skippy listened, his head numb and his body trembling. The house seemed to shake with the vibration of each step. To the frightened boys it sounded like a dirge, for the stairs creaked and groaned and the flooring, rotting with age and disuse, emitted eerie thumpings throughout the dismal house.

The darkness added much to their terrible fear, for they could not see each other and it had the effect of seeming to make them the more helpless. Skippy felt during those terrible seconds that he would not be able to raise a hand in his own defense.

So they waited, counting each heavy step and listening with increasing dread as they came nearer. It seemed to take an interminable time for those feet to span the distance between the top of the stairway and the door of their room. They squeezed each other's fingers tensely.

At last the footsteps ceased—not at their door, but across the hall!

Skippy gulped hard. Whoever it was, he was discovering that the door had been opened, the lock picked ... now he knew that his memorandum book was gone ... now he had noticed that the ladder had been taken from the closet.

They heard him rush out of the room and to the rear of the hall where they had left the ladder standing propped against the attic opening. Skippy could see the feeble glimmer of the lantern as it cast a lonely ray under their door.

Time stood still after that; they seemed to be in a state of suspended animation. Skippy could not hear Nickie breathe; Nickie listened in vain for a heart beat from Skippy's breast. The only sound that reached their ears was that of the rushing footsteps coming back now along the hall and suddenly stopping before their door.

Then the doorknob rattled.

The door did not give, of course; the bed was too tightly jammed against it. The boys waited and presently they knew that there was a desperate effort being made to open the door, for the bed vibrated from the impact. Finally there came a furious pounding on the oaken panel.

"Fallon—Kid?" the familiar, deep voice called insistently. "You boys there?"

Skippy felt then that his time had come.

CHAPTER XXIII

NICKIE REASONS

"You deaf?" came the funereal query. "Who's in there?"

Nickie was gulping audibly, but he could not speak. Skippy was forced to do something about it though every instinct within him rebelled against opening that door to Devlin. He pressed Nickie's hand, then released it and sat up straight.

"Huh? Who—who's there?" he asked, feigning sleepiness.

"Me—Barker! Who'd you think?" was the harsh reply. Then: "What's holding this door—*open it!*"

Skippy stepped out of the bed on feet of ice. "A m-m-minute," he said, in a quivering voice. "J-J-just a-a minute."

Nickie seemed urged into action too. He jumped out and sprang to Skippy's side. "No matter what, kid," he gasped quickly, "you'n me are pals—see? It's him or us n' we'll stick! You do the talkin' an' I'll watch his mitts. He's a big guy but there's two against one!"

"Yes," breathed Skippy, and together they pulled the bed away from the panel. As the door flew open, Devlin stood partly in the shadow, his face black with wrath. His eyes, so light and staring, seemed now to be on the verge of popping out of his long, narrow head, and his beetle brows were all but obscured by the straggling wisps of his unkempt hair.

"What's the big idea, eh?" he demanded, glaring at the boys and then at the bed.

His voice sounded almost like a clap of thunder and all Skippy could do was to look at the man's enormous feet. He had never noticed them before and they fascinated him.

"Have you lost your voices, *eh?*" Devlin roared. "*Answer me!*" There was no mistaking his anger.

"Gee whiz, mister—a—," Skippy stammered, "we was sound asleep n' all of a sudden we heard you poundin' on the door an'...."

"Shut up and answer my question! What's the idea of the bed against the door? What's the idea of Frost gone? The lock picked and the room ransacked?"

"We didn't touch nothin' but the ladder, mister," Skippy answered, feeling more courage. "We don't know nothin' bout the lock—it was like that when we come upstairs looking for a ladder. We wanted sump'n to do so we thought we'd go up in the attic n' look round 'cause it's fun on a rainy night an'...."

"Where's Frost gone?" It was like the roar of a lion.

Skippy cringed inwardly but he managed to smile in Devlin's face. "He just went, that's all. He said he left a note explainin' things an' he said somethin' about losin' his keys an' he was lookin' all round for 'em. Then he went upstairs n' he was up a long time an' then he come down."

"A lot of good you are!" Devlin rumbled deep in his throat. "What's the matter with you, Fallon—can't you talk any more, eh?"

"The kid's tellin' what happened, Dev——"

It was out!

Devlin glared. "Who told you to call me that?"

"Timmy told us Frost called you that." Nickie too, was quite calm now.

"He did, did he?" The man's eyes narrowed. "Well, let it pass, it don't matter now—this is my last month in this house, anyway, and no dick will hear that I'm Devlin through...." He stopped, as if bewildered, but only for a moment. Then he asked: "Which one of the Greeks did he take?"

"Both," Skippy said quietly.

"*Both!*" Devlin was plainly beside himself and he made no further attempt to conceal it. He stepped back into the hall, waving his long arms from side to side. "He did, did he! So he took 'em both, eh? Well, I'll show ... where's the note?"

"How'd we know?" Skippy retorted. "We looked for a ladder, that's all, n' it wouldn't be where there was a note, would it?"

If Devlin heard that, he gave no sign. He stalked into his room and was even then in possession of the note. While he read it, he ran his long, hairy fingers back and forth through his hair.

"His hair's wet, kid—awful wet!" Nickie whispered.

Skippy nodded grimly. "An' his feet, Nick—look at 'em—they're covered with mud! Looks like he's been walkin' through plenty."

Nickie shivered, but they said no more for Devlin had already read the note and was tearing it into a hundred pieces. Also, he was looking at the boys and a hard, cold glitter was in his eyes.

"You boys still haven't told me what you had the bed up against the door for?" he asked, with a hint of cunning in his suddenly modulated tones.

Skippy was quick to sense this and he gathered his wits to match Devlin's. Naïvely, he answered: "Maybe it's sissy-like for guys to get scared, mister, but we was never so scared as we was tonight when we was up in that attic. We was lookin' through one of those old trunks and all of a sudden we heard somebody runnin'."

"Yeah, runnin' like nobuddy's business," Nickie added, with narrowed eyes upon Devlin. "An' like he told us in his dream, who do we see standin' down there like a ghost, but Timmy!"

Devlin's face looked almost black, but he said nothing.

"Yeah, we was scared, an' how!" Skippy said excitedly. "It was rainin' so hard an' the wind was blowin' so we couldn't hear hardly nothin' he said."

"You couldn't?" Devlin's query was almost too eager.

Nickie sighed with understanding and Skippy went on, "All we heard him say was somethin' bout somebody bein' hurt. Maybe it was him, I don't know. Anyway, mister, we told him we couldn't let him in 'cause Frost was away an' we told him he better run an' go back where he come from. So he stood there awhile an' said sump'n about a car stoppin' an' all of a sudden the wind blew our lantern out 'cause we opened the window an' couldn't shut it again."

"Yeah, an' Timmy musta went away then," Nickie finished. "The kid an' me we calls n' calls so after I says to the kid, maybe we only imagined it was Timmy, hah? We been talkin' so much bout the nightmare he had that night, I says I guess we had it on the brain. It was some spooky here tonight with the storm an' all, an' a guy can imagine a lot."

"You must have imagined a terrible lot!" Devlin said gravely. "The last I saw of Timmy Underwood, he was waving to me from the window of a train bound for Montana."

Skippy stood speechless and Nickie walked helplessly to the bed and sat down.

"I suppose the whole thing made you a little nervous," Devlin said, staring down at the dilapidated writing table. He coughed. "This is a quiet place, specially during a storm. But boys your age being so nervous as to push the bed...."

"We couldn't find no match to light a lantern," Skippy said, feeling limp.

"Yeah, an' I didn't want no spooks creepin' in on me," Nickie added. "Live ones, I ain't afraid of...."

"Nonsense! The best thing you boys can do is to go to bed and forget it. I'm a little tired myself." After a pause, he added: "I'm taking you boys, somewhere in the morning so wake up early. Goodnight!"

Skippy couldn't get the door closed quickly enough. He threw himself on the bed exhausted. "Am I glad that's over!"

"Same here, kid," Nickie agreed in a faint voice. "Our little date with him tomorra ain't worryin' me like what Frost's gonna say bout that lock when he gets back."

"Keep your shirt on. From what Devlin's looked an' from what he ain't said about Frost, makes me think there'll be plenty trouble between *them* so the lock won't look big. Anyway, we can deny it, can't we? Frost's double-crossed Devlin a little, I think, so will Devlin believe all he says again, huh? Our word's as good as Frost's."

"Kid, I'm a dumb-bell again, ain't I? While you're makin' the old bean work I'm worryin' bout Devlin's mitts." Suddenly he lowered his voice still more and whispered close to Skippy's ear, "What's the idea sayin' we didn' hear nothin' that Timmy said?"

"We gotta outsmart *him*! While he thinks we ain't on to nothin', he won't be so foxy. Take it from me, Nickie, if we tell him nothin' we got a chance—not unless."

"What a guy!"

"If he thought we thought there was really sump'n phoney bout him an' Timmy tonight, we couldn't breathe no more without him knowin' it. He's gonna be foxy anyhow, but he'd be worse if he knew what we was thinkin' an' I betcha I'm right."

"You didn't fall for that about him seein' Timmy off on that train for Montana, hah?"

"We seen Timmy down in the clearin'—we seen him with our own eyes, didn' we?"

"Devlin looked like a minister when he said he seen Timmy wavin' on that, train. Could a guy be lyin' an' look like that?"

"That's why they call him Dean," Skippy murmured, thinking of what Carlton Conne had told him of the man's record. "He fools people 'cause he looks like a saint. Sure, he can lie—he don't do nothin' else but."

"It's awful, kid, but I can't think what we saw was real—*it couldn't be*!"

"But the mud on his shoes an' his wet hair...." Skippy argued.

And when day dawned warm and clear, they had come no nearer to the truth than that.

CHAPTER XXIV

WAITING

Devlin had a change of mind during the intervening hours, and at breakfast he announced with his usual gravity that they would not make the trip that day after all. He had some important business to attend to first, he said, and would leave them alone that afternoon. On Monday evening they would go.

He seemed not at all concerned about the attic but just before he was leaving that afternoon, he started to remove the ladder.

"Aw, leave it there, won't you?" Skippy asked imploringly. "Nickie an' me, we get sick of the dark rooms downstairs an' up there we can play cards an' all without a light. Gee whiz...."

Skippy won.

Devlin's cold, staring eyes glittered more than ever after he gave his consent and there was a calm about him when he went out that left the boys perplexed.

They rushed to the window when they heard him slam the metal door of the woodshed. Eagerly they watched while he stalked with measured steps toward the barn. Then they saw him backing out slowly in a blue coupe that was distinctly second-hand.

"Another car!" Nickie gasped.

"Gee, I expected it, an' I didn't!" was Skippy's comment. "Did we hear Timmy say that old sedan went over into the lake, or didn't we?"

"We did *and how*! You're right, kid, it looks like I'm goofey about that spook stuff. We won't argue about it no more. What we gonna do all day, hah?"

"Work on those bars," Skippy grinned. "Gee whiz, Nick, tell the truth, I didn't think we'd have the chance. I thought he had us where he wanted."

Seven hours later, they were not so sure but that Devlin would be triumphant after all. They had worked sedulously during that time but there was only a little give in the top bar and the boys were well nigh discouraged.

Sitting atop the trunk they surveyed the bars ruefully. Another day was drawing to its close, another day that brought them nearer to the Fate which only Devlin held the key to. Skippy felt weary and sick.

"There's no use, I guess, Nick. It's comin' out like Timmy said—we can't do a thing till he takes us outa here for our turn."

"Yeah, then we gotta use our beans an' scram. But it's got *me*, kid; we saw in that book how much money he expects from us. How can he get it when we're dead?"

"I dunno. We ain't gonna hash this mystery business all over again—I'm too blamed tired. All I'm sure of is that Devlin gets money for us an' sometime or other he'll wanta kill us for some reason. Timmy said it was a trick about him shippin' us west, so that's the night he does it—always at night, you know that. When that night comes for us, we just gotta outguess him."

"An' it's about a month from the time he takes us to a sawbones," Nickie said mournfully. "Well, if we can't do nothin' else about it, I'm gonna pull myself together. But one thing, I hope he takes us together— see. If you go first or I go—holy smoke, I can't stand it if he takes us separate. I'm scared I'll lose my nerve—you know it?"

"Forget it, Nick. Whatever he does, be foxy an' forget about me n' I'll do the same. Gee whiz, from what Timmy said he don't tie you down—if he did that we wouldn't have a chance. Now quit worryin', an' let's get down before he comes. I'll hide the things again an' maybe he'll be out a lotta the time an' we can try it again. If we keep pullin' on them bars we'll weaken 'em after awhile even if it's weeks."

"Yeah, weeks too late."

Nickie's spirits rose considerably a little later. Devlin had come in with a pail of chicken fricassee and an apple pie, announcing that he had stopped at a lunch wagon to give the boys a treat. Skippy almost decided that all his suspicions had been unfounded.

The problem was a tormenting one. Could anyone be so cruel? Devlin's face, always a study, was no nearer revealing what lay behind his grave features than on the day they had first seen him. Just now he was as much absorbed in the chicken fricassee as the boys were.

A full stomach does much toward comforting the harassed human being, and Nickie was no exception to the rule. The keen look of defiance came back into his eyes and he settled back in his chair, quite forgetting for the time that the man who had so generously fed him, was the man whom he had expected would kill him.

Skippy's full stomach, while giving him much comfort, did not disarm him completely. He sat back in his chair, noting Nickie's peaceful face beside him and Devlin's mask-like countenance across the table. Someone had to be ready and on guard—Devlin had a price for everything—even chicken fricassee.

It came sooner than he expected. Devlin was finishing his pie and washing it down with great draughts of coffee. "Well, boys," he said, genially, "I suppose both of you swim, eh?"

Skippy kicked Fallon under the table and said, "Nope, not a stroke—neither of us. Do we, Nick?"

"Nah. Ain't it a shame, hah? We oughta."

"Yes, yes. It's something every boy ought to know." Devlin got up and his bulk seemed greater than ever. His face had resumed its thoughtful expression and the glitter had returned to his eyes. "Well, I'll be going up now—a little business I got to attend to. If you boys wash up the dishes you can have a game of cards before bedtime, eh?"

They listened as he walked through the hall and up the stairs. Skippy waited until he heard the man's step in his own room before he said, "Well, he's begun workin' on us all right, an' I trumped his ace right off the bat."

"How, kid?"

"He expected us to say we could swim."

"How did...."

"'cause I'm layin' for him all the time from now on. Whatever he expected to do if we'd said yes, I don't know. But I know, he's aimin' to try the car trick on us an' he wanted to make sure things wouldn't go wrong. He can't afford to have us not drown when he's countin' on it, can he?"

Nickie put his elbows on the table and cupped his chin. "You mean we gotta go through with it an' take the chance that he can't kill us 'cause we can swim?"

"If there ain't any other chance, we gotta."

"Well, I'm licked!" Nickie said hopelessly.

But he wasn't ... not yet....

CHAPTER XXV

A PASSING FACE

Distrustful though they were and full of nameless fears, they stepped into Devlin's coupé early on Monday evening with a feeling of relief. To be out in the air again, a part of the moving, restless world—it gave them no small thrill and they tried to put out of their minds all that had troubled them since their strange imprisonment.

Devlin, adept at using either hand, dexterously managed the car with his left hand and kept his right hand significantly at his pocket. "I might as well warn you boys," he said when they had left the clearing, "that I'll stand for no nonsense. I got a silencer on this gun in my pocket and it won't make any noise if either one of you try to beat it."

Nickie seemed to have been silenced without the gun, but Skippy said, "Aw, don't worry, mister. Why should we beat it when you're gonna ship us out west an' everything, huh?"

"I'm glad you feel that way," the man said gravely, but watching the boys out of the corner of his eye. "Timmy got very restless waiting around and I had an idea he was putting notions in your heads." He coughed.

"Aw, no," Skippy said with a gulp. "I—er—he didn't say nothin'."

Devlin did not relax. "I might as well tell you my plans now," he said slowly. "I'm taking you both to a country doctor not far from here for a physical examination. You are to act as if you didn't know where you were born or much of anything else—understand? You may answer yes and no to any questions he asks you but that is all. I'll do the rest of the talking. And you're my sons—my sons! Don't forget that for a moment. I'll be watching every minute."

They rode through the woods path, turning here and there so that Skippy could not keep track of the route. Dusk was rapidly approaching and when Devlin slowed down the car as they came abreast of a narrow path, he could just about make it out.

Devlin stopped the car and got out backwards. Then, reaching in the pocket flap of the coupé door, he drew out a searchlight and played it up and down the boggy-looking path for a flashing second, yet giving Skippy plenty of time to notice several large footprints on both sides of the trail.

He said nothing to Nickie for Devlin was back in the car again in a moment and they had started off. A few feet farther on they crossed a tiny wooden bridge of amateur construction.

"Frost and me fixed that up," said the man as they rattled over the logs. He coughed again. "Part bog and part creek and about fifteen feet deep where we put the logs. Nasty place. Folks around here don't know anything about it any more—their grandfolks and great-grandfolks that did have forgot about it now."

They came at last to a road that had once boasted asphalt and Skippy guessed that it had taken them at least an hour to reach it. Along this they speeded silently, each one wrapped in his own thoughts. Not a car did they meet, not a person or house did they pass and it was fully two hours after they had left the dismal house when they espied a small, lighted dwelling by the roadside.

Devlin drove past that, too, and presently he turned on to another badly paved road which took them uphill. Skippy noticed the dark outline of mountains spreading out around them. It was true then, he thought, the house was situated in the center of swamplands and forest. But where—where were they?

Another half hour's ride and they came into a small village, boasting a few stores and not more than twenty-five houses. It was at the extreme end of this quiet community and a little around the bend that Devlin brought the car to a stop.

"Here we are," he said, backing out as soon as he had turned off his switch. "Now remember—leave the talking to me!"

Skippy felt the gun at his back all the way up the graveled walk. Nickie kept safely ahead and walked with short, jerky steps. They went up on the porch and a pleasant-faced lady answered the doorbell.

She led them into the sitting room at Devlin's deep-voiced request, and then disappeared. Then the doctor appeared, a short, near-sighted little man who talked in nasal accents and put his stethoscope to Skippy's rapidly beating heart with professional alacrity.

"So you got here, eh," he said, as he changed the instrument about on the boy's chest. "Mr. Smithson told me you'd come. Name's Barker, eh? Well, must say you're a sensible man to watch out what's ahead. Guess both boys'll pass muster. So you're starting a mushroom place down at Devil's Bog, eh?"

"Yes, yes," Devlin answered, standing in a nonchalant posture near the door. "Know much about it, doc?"

"No, nothing, except that it's full of malaria and mosquitoes and a dangerous place to go unless a body knows where they're going," the garrulous man answered. "I've never been there—guess your place is quite a ways in, eh?"

"Mm," Devlin answered. "Beggars can't be choosers, doc. I got to do the best I can for my boys."

The doctor snorted. "Guess that's so. Sometimes they don't thank a body any." He had disposed of Skippy by that time and nodded to Nickie. "Just keep your eye on 'em, that's all you can do." Then: "Did you say they're going to help you?"

"Mm, I'm too poor to get anyone else."

And that was all. The doctor dismissed them, saying he had to get out on a call and before Skippy could think what to do, they were out on the porch and the door had closed behind them. Nickie looked at his friend, desperately.

Skippy sat down on the bottom step and began to untie his shoe. "Something's hurtin' my foot, mister," he said innocently, as Devlin stood above him, tall and questioning. "Guess it's the lining—wait a minute!"

Devlin walked a few feet away, standing in an advantageous position while his staring eyes darted from one boy to the other. Then, impatiently, he walked on to the car. "I'm watching you, kid—hurry!" he said, after curtly ordering Nickie inside.

Skippy got his shoe back on and began to saunter slowly down the walk, when suddenly he saw someone turn in at the path. His heart jumped! It was a lady and from under her hat the boy could see white hair. God had sent her!

"I'm waiting, kid!"

Devlin's voice was icy. Skippy had to think quickly and, consequently, there was a sharp contact, the lady's pocketbook fell to the ground and its contents fell out on the walk.

Skippy was nothing if not gallant. He was on his knees, picking up the scattered articles and cramming them back despite her sweet-voiced protests. But he had to do it quickly, expertly, for Devlin had a challenging look in his cold eyes.

Then he ran to the car and Nickie gave him an anxious look. "Sorry I hadda keep you waitin', mister," he said naïvely, "but that lady was old an' she couldn't stoop so well so I …"

"Come on, get in!" was Devlin's response.

Skippy looked back and saw that the old lady stood holding her pocketbook tightly, watching them as they drove away. Then she went up the walk to the doctor's house.

After they had gone a few feet, Devlin backed the car around and went back the way they had come. As they drove down the brightly lighted street of the little community, they came abreast of a car which as Skippy had already noticed bore a New York license plate. Even while he looked, a face at one of the opened windows drew his attention, a brisk face so pleasantly familiar.

Dick Hallam!

He tried to stifle his cry of surprise, but Devlin had not missed it. "You know the man in that car?" He had already stepped on the gas and they were plunging forward with terrific speed. "You know him?" he asked, insistently, threateningly.

"Y—yes."

Skippy saw the headlights looming up from the rear. Dick Hallam was giving chase. He had seen him! Devlin, on the other hand, was not dismayed. He was using all the speed of which the car was capable and had turned off all except his parking lights. Suddenly he swerved into a narrow road and after that they made so many turns that Skippy lost all sense of direction.

When Devlin slowed down he coughed with satisfaction. "I'm glad to see that neither of you tried to pull a fast one. I had made up my mind that I'd wreck the car if you did—I'm that way, boys."

"Yeah, we can see that," Nickie said, with no conscious attempt to be humorous. "You needn't a' worried bout me, Devlin—I wouldn't a' laid a hand on you. The shave was close enough the way this car was goin'."

Skippy had barely heard anything that was said. He could think only that Dick Hallam had been near enough to touch not a half hour back, and now the night, and perhaps Death itself, separated them. Certainly, it was too much to hope that Hallam should find them now or ever!

The doctor had said that no one knew of Devil's Bog. Why hadn't he known the name of the place before? Neither Carlton Conne nor his men would ever find the place from his poor description of it. And yet, he thought, did not the desolate swampland stand out from all other swamplands? Somehow, it did.

And Dean Devlin, known or unknown, made it stand out still more.

CHAPTER XXVI

GOLDEN OPPORTUNITY

They talked it all over before they went to sleep that night and concluded that one bright star of hope burned brightly in their favor. Everything indicated that Devlin meant to get them both off his hands at once. Nickie observed that perhaps Frost had put the idea in his head and, if so, they had much for which to thank him.

Skippy's thoughts were full of Dick Hallam and he dared to think there might be some hope in that direction. Might not Hallam guess that Devlin was holding him prisoner somewhere in the locality? Might not Carlton Conne send out his men to scour the countryside until they trailed down the forgotten house that lay in the fastnesses of Devil's Bog?

"He's gotta!" Skippy said aloud.

"Hah?" Nickie asked sleepily.

"I was tellin' myself that sump'n's gotta come our way. That guy we passed—I know him. He'll use his head that we must be some place nearby an' he'll have a hunt started for us."

"Yeah, but we're a coupla hours' ride from where the sawbones lives."

"It's called Hillbriar—I seen it on a sign."

"Yeah, and this place—*Devil's Bog!* That's a swell monicker all right. It's the right place for Devlin all right. If the *n* was out an' the *i* put before the *l* they could call him The Devil of Devil's Bog, hah? Say, the more I think the worse headache I get about that doctor business. He ain't in on Devlin's racket, that's a cinch. If only Devlin didn't pack that rod, kid, we coulda spilled things. But he was watchin' us close, the dirty rat."

"Yeah, an' I wasn't gonna take no chance neither. Gee whiz, Nickie, we're better off waitin' 'cause it's better bein' alive than go off the handle an' have maybe three of us dead. Then he coulda skipped out an' nobody woulda heard a shot."

"Yeah, we didn't have no chance without gettin' blowed up. Even in the car, that rat wasn't missin' no tricks. A coupla times I was gonna give you a sign, 'cause I thought between us, we could land on him, but he had that silencer right in his mitt. He ain't got no feelin's, he makes me thinka rock with icy water tricklin' down it."

"Did you notice anythin' just before we come to the creek, Nickie? I mean when he stopped an' got out with his flash?"

Nickie lifted himself up on his elbow. "Say," he whispered, "them footsteps? Say, I was wonderin' too. What was in there that he was so nosey about, hah?"

"Wish I knew, believe me. That path I betcha goes through the woods an' down to that bog. He said, didn't he, that the creek an' the bog both wound round that way, huh? Anyway, it's a cinch that he was down that path Saturday night. We seen mud on his feet an' tonight we could see his footsteps."

"Then it looks like he took Timmy for ..." Nickie whispered fearfully.

"I been thinkin' the same thing. Gee whiz, Nickie, it's awful, huh? He's like you say—a devil! We gotta be pretty foxy with a feller like that. He ain't afraida nothin', I don't think."

"Yeah, an' don't think we can beat him to it. Lissen, kid, he's twice our size an' the gun he carries ain't no water pistol. It looks like if he don't get us one way, he'll get us the other. Kid, the only way we'll get a break is for your friends to round up the dicks an' come down here and surprise Devlin. An' how can that happen when they don't know...."

"But maybe they will, Nickie," Skippy whispered hopefully. "I didn't know the name of this place when I wrote that note. Even I didn't have a chance to hardly get it outa my shoe so I wouldn't a' had a chance...."

"An' that old lady," Nickie interposed ruefully. "Holy Smoke, kid, what a chance that was to slip her that note if Devlin hadn't kep' watchin' every move. Just the kinda old lady we was talkin' about too."

"What you talkin' about, Nickie, huh?"

"That note what you was gonna slip the first old lady you could— remember? An' you'd a' had a swell break if it wasn't for Devlin. He's a hoodoo with that funeral pan o' his."

"Gee whiz, Nickie, did I get away with it as swell as that? Gosh, I was scared skinny that maybe Devlin was wise I knocked her pocketbook outa her hand on purpose. *She* didn't know I did it on purpose."

"On purpose—how come?"

"Sure, I thought you knew it, Nickie. Gee whiz, was that a break that it opened up an' her stuff ran all over the walk! When I give it back that note was inside."

"Kid, that's the pay-off! If that ain't a break."

"Well, I did an' how! By now I bet she's read that an' maybe already she's put it in an envelope an' it's on the way to New York."

Skippy would not have been able to endure the anxiety of the following days if he had not had faith that the note was well on its way. Hope would soon have fled if he had known that the sweet-voiced old lady had not discovered the note that night, nor for many nights to come. She had gone home after her visit to the doctor and, being confined to her bed for the next two weeks with a bad cold, there had been no occasion to use her "best" pocketbook.

Devlin seemed destined to win.

CHAPTER XXVII

ACCUSATIONS

Their hopes flared high, then burned so low that they were beginning to exchange whispers of despair. When a week had passed, then ten days, they looked at each other hopelessly and each knew what was in the other's thoughts without the exchange of a word. Timmy's "nerves" had been nothing compared to Nickie's "jumpiness," as he called it. He fairly quailed whenever Devlin's footsteps sounded.

The man kept to his own room, except for three consecutive days when he left the house just before dusk and returned late at night. At those times, the boys hurried to the attic and fell to work at the window bars, only to realize at the end of the week, that it would take more than their inadequate little pot handle to gain freedom.

On Wednesday of the following week, Devlin was plainly angry. The boys knew he was thinking of Frost and they seemed to sense that the man's unexpected departure was enraging Devlin more and more. He paced the length of the house, muttering to himself and clenching his big hands until his knuckles cracked. This continued throughout the afternoon.

Supper was a disappointment as all the meals had been. Devlin had not again been so generous as to surprise them with any more of the lunchroom delicacies such as he had brought in on that Sunday night. Meal after meal was the same, a monotony of canned beans, bacon and crackers.

Skippy had no appetite that night. The smell of bacon made him sick and he felt that never again in his life would he be able to eat it. Nickie moped dejectedly over his plate and when he did put anything to his mouth he washed it down quickly with coffee as if he dared not taste it.

He looked at Skippy and shook his head. "If there's two more weeks like this, kid, you'll need your strength—see. I'm sick, too, but I feel I gotta eat no matter what, so I wash every mouthful down with this rotten coffee. No matter how rotten coffee is, it's better'n tastin' them blamed beans and bacon."

Skippy was trying out this sound advice when they heard the familiar sound of a car chugging into the clearing. Nickie put down his coffee cup with a bang and before either one of them could make any comment, they heard Devlin rushing out of his room and down the stairway.

He came loping into the kitchen muttering, "Frost—it's Frost," and rushed to one of the windows and looked out.

The boys were at the other window in a second and though the evening shadows were lengthening, they could see the big, dark car rolling into the barn. They watched as Frost came out with his short, hopping stride, and they heard Devlin mumble deep in his throat.

The man made no attempt to go near the door but stood back against the wall and waited. The boys went back to the table and made a pretense of drinking their coffee. All the time, however, they too were waiting and they listened intently as Frost's key clinked against the metal door.

Abruptly his leathern-looking face appeared in the doorway wreathed in smiles. "Howdy!" he was saying breezily. "How——" He caught the insane glint in Devlin's eyes and stood suddenly still. "Say, you don't look glad to see me, boss!"

"Did you expect me to?" Devlin's voice boomed through the room.

Frost flushed up to the roots of his colorless hair. His small, shifty eyes strayed toward the boys, then back to Devlin again. "Oh, if you feel that way about it—I was thinkin' I was helpin' you out—givin' you a hand...."

"Since when did I ask you to do my thinking for me, eh? Since when did you give me a hand without being told to?" There was a ring in Devlin's voice that made his listeners quiver when he added, "Come upstairs—I've got plenty to say to you!"

The boys had never had any doubt that Devlin was a man of his word. Now they were learning that he went far beyond that and gave no quarter to anyone who had taken too much for granted at his expense. And from the terrible wrath with which Devlin shook the house, Frost must have been aware that he had committed the unforgivable sin in the eyes of his nefarious employer.

Devlin seemed to have thrown aside all caution in his anger. His solemn, terrible voice trailed down the stairs to where the boys were standing, absorbing it all. Frost, at first, had made a feeble protest, but was soon forced to stand back and listen.

"Boss," he had said, obsequiously, "there ain't no use gettin' sore when I only meant to help out. Anyways, it seemed like wastin' time stayin' here and...."

"*Shut up!*"

Devlin's long, determined stride shook the floor with each step he took. "I didn't make up my mind what to do about those infernal Greek kids. And I had that pest Timmy on my hands while you...."

"Didn't things blow right, Boss?" Frost's voice sounded conciliatory.

Devlin shouted, "Don't remind me of it! I tell you it looks like luck is turning against me. First with Tucker out in Chi and now Timmy—I tell you they're a dead loss! Then I come in here Saturday night almost dead, I'm so tired, and what do I find! You gone on your own hook with the two Greeks—after me telling you to stay here!"

"But, Boss—I did the job without no trouble and...."

"With that grinning face of yours I suppose you could look the part, eh? Only I've got the face for this business—people don't get wise to a face like mine—they think I'm drowning in grief. But *you*—I wasn't going to let you go through with the Greeks; either one of 'em. I decided that when I was fooled by that pest of a Timmy. It's risky enough for me without you going ahead and doing things on your own. It shows what brains you've got when you couldn't even wait the month at least."

Frost became sullen and defiant at this challenge. "Oh, yeah?" he parried. "Well, let me tell *you* somethin', Boss. I was goin' to tell you when I come in but you ain't give me a chance to get a word in—I had brains to wait a month all right, but somethin' happened. We got a room and I passed the word around we was looking for jobs like you work it. I even give the landlady such a sob story she gives me the dope herself that we ought to get our names on the dotted line so it was soft."

"How much?" Devlin inquired almost eagerly.

"A grand each!" came the proud reply. "I made the agent talk me into that—he said a thousand when I said five hundred."

"Go on!"

"I made the first payment Friday, and Saturday morning we went out after dawn for a fishing trip—not a phoney one, Boss—I meant it real 'cause I wanted the low down on how I'd work it when the time was ripe. I knew by then they couldn't swim, but like I say it was a try-out. It was a hazy morning and the water was rough and we hadn't got far out when that Shorty stands up in the boat to pass something to Biff. Next thing I know we was in the water and the Greeks was shoutin' their heads off and the tide was pushin' me down-stream like anything. I couldn't swim against it and I was lucky to grab the end of the boat that was floatin' upside down. Anyway, a guy fishin' in near shore hears the racket and comes out. But the Greeks had got it and he was lucky to help me."

"Did they find 'em?" Devlin's question was eager.

"Sure, and say, wasn't I plastered with sympathy at that boardin' house! Things just blew my way. I won't have no trouble gettin' the money. In three weeks I'm going back and collect. I told 'em out there that I was comin' East to look for work 'cause the trouble didn't make Pittsburgh look so good to me."

"That's better, Frost—I didn't think you had it in you. Those two downstairs will be off my hands by that time—I'll go out with you."

"I wouldn't take no chances if I was you, Boss. I got today's papers in the car. They're playin' up on the Delafield kids and they hinted there was a racket behind it!"

"*What?*" Devlin's heavy foot pounded on the floor.

"Yeah," Frost answered as if he were almost enjoying the telling of it, "one paper says the dicks are hep and some famous detective has promised to run down the brains of it."

"*Carlton Conne!*" was all Devlin said.

"That's what I thought right away. You know that guy, Boss, so I'd lay off a little. You might get jammed in Pittsburgh. I can collect them two G's all right."

"I realize that, Frost," said Devlin coldly. "But trouble or no trouble, I'm going to go to Pittsburgh with *you—understand?*"

The boys could not hear Frost's reply. He might not have voiced his opinion at all. But Devlin's heavy steps overhead seemed to speak volumes. Suddenly he hurled a question that made Skippy's heart stand still.

"Frost," he was shouting, "where's that memorandum book of mine, eh?"

The boys sprang into the kitchen. They closed the door noiselessly behind them and sat down, stunned and hopeless looking.

"Well, it's come, hah?"

Skippy nodded. "Gee whiz, I did forget. We just gotta deny it like we planned."

"Yeah, but that ain't sayin' Devlin's gonna believe us, kid."

Skippy leaned forward on the table, his eyes blinking thoughtfully. "Listen, Nickie, it don't make no difference what he believe, does it? If we don't get help, we'll have to go with him an' take the chance like we planned. So we should worry about it either way."

Skippy was right. Worrying about it wouldn't help. Devlin and Frost came downstairs a few minutes later and accused them, but they managed to stick to their guns. That they had taken the ladder seemed to have caused no suspicion; neither had the boys' frequent trips to the attic revealed how desperate had been their efforts to loosen the bars. Devlin seemed not to have noticed it.

His mind was on the notebook and his face showed that he would not dismiss the topic easily. "Where is it?" he was saying.

"Say, mister, what do we want with a darn old notebook anyway!" Skippy retorted. "Search us—search our whole room but you won't find it, 'cause what would we want with it, huh?"

"That's what I'd like to know," Devlin said, narrowing his eyes. He turned to Nickie, "I think you picked that lock—what for?"

"Aw, pipe down. Even if I did—what about it, hah? You can see that we didn't take anything an' if we had, what could we do with it? I guess you ain't worried that we got any money or anything like that, hah?"

"Hear that, Frost? I guess they're telling the truth and that puts it up to you. You trying to double cross me?"

"Say, I ain't that dumb, Boss," Frost protested. "Maybe you mislaid it or lost it."

"Maybe—and maybe not." Then Devlin turned on his heel and left the room with Frost hopping after him protesting his innocence. But it was evident to the boys that Devlin suspected Frost for the dour looking leader returned soon muttering: "I'll get him yet."

CHAPTER XXVIII

THE MICE WILL PLAY

It was apparent next day that relations were strained between the two men. Frost went about looking sullen and defiant and Devlin, when he was not up in his room sleeping, sat in the kitchen drinking coffee with ominous gravity.

Late afternoon came and Devlin appeared dressed to go out. He strode about the kitchen several times, then walked to the door. Frost eyed him curiously.

"Goin' out, Boss?" he asked.

Devlin looked back and nodded. "I'll be back early tonight." He glanced at the boys. "You be ready to take a ride with Frost and me."

He slammed the door and Nickie paled, noticeably. Frost sat idly at the table drumming his thick fingers upon the oilcloth cover. Skippy went to the window and watched until Devlin backed the big car out. Then he turned suddenly.

"Say, mister," he said to Frost, "me an' Nickie know what Devlin'll take us on a ride for tonight."

If Frost was surprised he did not show it. He glanced up at Skippy. "So you're a wise kid, hey?"

"Nope, we just kept our ears open last night an' heard plenty. Devlin talked loud enough so we put two and two together. Anyhow we know Timmy never went out West—we know he's dead. Tucker got picked up in Chicago an' that put the bulls wise Devlin was in a new racket."

Frost was aghast. "How do you—you...."

Skippy put his cards on the table. "I know everthin' now, I do, an' I knew plenty before I ever seen Devlin. We'll give you a break if you let us get away tonight. If you don't Devlin'll go to Pittsburgh with you an' grab that dough—a blind guy could see he figures you're givin' him the double-x—an' besides I heard him say he'd get you. Anyhow I know the cops'll grab him there an' if you're with him you'll be grabbed, too. So chaw on that a bit."

Frost was plainly frightened. "He's been actin' so crazy lately he might take me for a ride at that and if I get grabbed with him I'll get the hot squat too."

Skippy used the best thrust he knew. "Sure, you will. The cops got that notebook right now—anyway if they ain't, Carlton Conne's got it an' that's as good as with the cops." He waited a moment until that shot had found its mark and then he added: "I sent Carlton Conne a note an' that notebook too the night Devlin took us to the doctor's house—I told him how long it was from the time we had the accident an' all about this house an' what the hermit told you. So if you know anything about Carlton Conne you know he'll find this joint sooner or later an' if Nickie an' me are dead, it'll be tough for you if you're found with Devlin. Now I'll give you a break if you'll give us one. How 'bout it?"

Like many of his ilk, Frost thought only of his own safety and as he had neither brains nor cunning, he did not stop to question nor consider anything but himself.

"Sure, I'll give you kids a break—*sure!*" he was crying like the yellow creature he was. "You think I wanta burn with Devlin when I ain't done nothin' yet but help kids for him, hey? I met him in Chi and he brought me here and propositioned me. But I ain't never tried the trick on any kids and them Greeks if they didn't get drowned like they did, I couldn't gone through with it—I know it. I got more feelin's than Devlin, but I hadda stick and play up—get me? I come along in a car that night I see him first and saw him ship that Tucker kid over that cliff into the lake. I'd made a stick-up a few minutes before and I was makin' my getaway without lights."

"An' you seen what he did?" Skippy asked eagerly.

"Sure. He didn't hear me and he didn't see me so I switched off under some trees and it was a lonesome road that hardly anybody traveled between midnight and morning. I see an old car stop and this guy gets out. It's Devlin. Then you could have knocked me over when I sees him give the little car a shove right over the cliff. So me bein' in a little racket myself I puts on my lights and chugs up to him and he waves me to stop. So he gives me a story that him and his son was ridin' along and the car stalls. He gets out to crank it while his son gets behind the wheel to fix the spark. Well, the brake mustn't been on, he tells me, when all of a sudden he sees the car headed right over the cliff to the lake. He just has time to jump out of the way, he says."

"Such a warm-hearted guy he is!" Nickie said disgustedly.

"Yeah, he ain't got no heart," Frost said, with more composure. "But to make it quick, I tell him I'm wise and what's his racket. So we get real chummy and he tells me to drive on and when we do he says it's insurance that he's working."

"*Insurance!*" Skippy repeated as if he must never forget the word.

"Yeah, he tells me it's a good payin' racket. He says he can get orphans so they don't have no real near folks inquirin' after 'em. He can get 'em insured and wait a month or so, then he can take 'em out in a car, an old closed car he likes to get that don't cost him more'n a few bucks—you know, the kind that's ready for the junk yard. If they can swim he can dope 'em a little with some stuff he's got so by the time they get where he wants, all he has to do is to get out and push the car over to the water."

"So that's how he worked it, huh?" Skippy asked, feeling rather sick.

"Sure," Frost answered readily. "If they can't swim, he likes it better. Then he uses that stallin' business to get out, leavin' off the brake. He thought he had Tucker sure, but the kid comes to and gets out in time so Devlin thinks he don't give him enough dope."

Nickie shuddered visibly. "So he reports it an accident?"

"Yeah, and with that funeral face Devlin gets away with it. When the whole business is over he collects the insurance."

"Gee whiz!" Skippy murmured. *"It's awful!"*

"Yeah, don't think I liked it when he told me!" Frost said, on the defensive. "But he told me I wouldn't have to do no part of that. He said all I had to do was the details like he called it. So what could I do when he had told me all that and asked me to come in on it with him? He'd have put me on the spot for what I knew about him if I didn't. Besides, he said it was goin' to be safe and that he'd worked it out so's we couldn't get caught."

"Why didn't you stay in Pittsburgh?" Skippy asked suddenly. "You wanted to, I betcha."

"Sure, I did. But he'da found me—if it was years he'd find me so I thought I'd better come back."

"You can go back to Pittsburgh tonight if you help us get away. You can start back now—the coupe's out in the barn, ain't it?"

"Yeah, but he might..." Frost began.

"Tell him you took us out for the air an' we beat it."

Nickie was aroused, jubilant at the new turn of events. "Yeah, an' say, Frost, tell him you chased us down in the woods where the bog gets tough, but that we give you the slip there, hah?"

"That's the stunt, Mister Frost. And tell him you'll hunt us on one side while he hunts on the other. Then, when he's gone, you beat it fast, 'cause we'll have the cops in here after him by that time. He can't chase you to Pittsburgh when he's in jail, can he?"

Frost fell as Skippy afterward termed it, "hook, line and sinker." "Sounds like it's fool-proof, kids," he said. "And the dicks don't know about me, hey?"

"How would they?" Skippy assured him.

Frost got up. "I'll get my keys," he said, "and we'll beat it pronto. I'll take you to the highway and make out I won't be glad to beat it."

Nickie looked at Skippy while they were waiting. "It ain't true you sent that notebook, is it?" he asked incredulously.

Skippy grinned. "Gee, *you're* not fool-proof, Nickie. How could I get that book without Devlin seein' me that night, huh? Didn't I have a big enough job on my hands gettin' that note into the old lady's pocketbook? I hadda spread it on thick to frighten him right off an' make him think the cops had that book—well, it ain't a lie exactly 'cause they'll have it some day an', boy, is that enough to send Devlin where he can't be sent any more, huh?"

"An' how!" Nickie agreed. "Then it's still out there behind the barrel, hah?"

"Sure, an' it's gonna stay there till the cops come an' get it. I'll tell 'em where it is—nobody else would think to look for it there. We can't let Frost see us takin' it now an' even if we could, I don't like it on us in case anythin' goes wrong."

"Aw, what could go wrong now, hah?" Nickie said confidently. "Frost takes us out to the road where we're safe, so we should worry."

Skippy felt somewhat less confident. He could not, try as he would, put away from him the feeling that nothing was sure in the dark, forgotten swampland of Devil's Bog. When they were once clear of it entirely, he told himself, he would be able to laugh at the fears which he felt now.

CHAPTER XXIX

A SLIP

Frost drove away from the clearing with a confidence that communicated itself to Nickie. He was talkative, affable and even informative. Devlin, he told them, had searched out the abandoned house after his talk with the old hermit when they had had a breakdown with their car some ten miles from the bog. Their hunt hadn't been an easy one—they made the journey three times before they found the place.

"But the boss is that persistent," the man was saying. "He don't give up. That's why I ast you kids to tell the dicks as soon's you get out, 'cause if he don't find you by tonight, he'll be hoppin' off after me."

"Did he tell you anything about poor Timmy, huh?" Skippy asked. "Did he tell you that he come back that night?"

"He didn't tell me nothin' about him excep' that he had trouble," Frost answered truthfully. "But I know what you kids think about it—I think the same thing. He said he could never go to Albany and collect on Timmy so you know what that means without me tellin'."

Skippy couldn't talk about it—it was all too horrifying. Nickie must have felt the same way for he was silent and his dark eyes kept to the narrow woods trail as if he dared not look on either side. Somewhere in that bog was Timmy, free from Devlin at last.

They rode along in silence after that and though they were all a bit nervous they felt that courage would come when a safe distance had been put between them and the terrible house. Though Devlin was not there in body he seemed to be there in spirit, and they longed to get out of the woods and into the open where he could no longer wield his power.

It was about five o'clock. Bits of warm sunshine filtered through the higher branches of the trees but below the shadows were gathering and where the growth was thick a gloom had already penetrated.

When they had been riding for some little time, Frost said, "The boss is goin' to see Smithson, the insurance man, I think. He lives in Hillbriar near that doctor you went to see. He must have some place else to go, I been thinkin', 'cause it wouldn't take him that long to just go there."

The boys were about to agree when they rounded a turn in the narrow trail and saw just ahead the path which Devlin had seemed so interested in on that memorable Monday night. Also, they saw Devlin sitting in his car as if he had just climbed in and was ready to start away. He was headed in the same direction that they were.

Frost swerved the car with such force that it almost turned on its side. "Scram, kids!" he said hoarsely. "I'll have to too! He'll know—he'll know I'm double-crossin' him!"

Skippy was out of the coupé with Nickie jumping after him. They grasped hands instinctively, and broke through the thick brush running blindly, wildly, but running as they had never run before. Devlin's terrible voice seemed to follow them everywhere for his shouts rang out time and again and they heard Frost scream several times.

Not once did they look back. They could hear the crackling brush and they thought that Frost must be somewhere in their wake. They thought no more about the man than that for they were too intent on their own preservation. They must not, at any cost, stop until Devlin's funereal echoes were left far behind.

Darkness had almost overtaken them before they had the courage to sit down and rest on a fallen log. Muddy and scratched from head to foot, they would have presented a comical picture if it had not been for the piteous expression on their faces. Mosquitoes had already got in some of their work as the great red lumps on their hands and foreheads indicated.

"We gotta slap mud on thick, Nickie," Skippy said wearily. "I read once about a kid what was lost in a swamp and he did that and saves his life. These blamed things can eat a feller up—you know it?"

"I feel like I'm ate up a'ready," Nickie answered pathetically. "Kid, you think we gotta stay in this graveyard all night?"

"It's night now an' where are we? There's no use stumblin' 'round in the dark, is there? We might walk plunk into that bog an' you heard yourself what Frost said about it. You don't get out once you walk into some parts."

"Wonder where Frost is, hah? I don't remember when we stopped hearin' him behind us. I s'pose we oughta stopped, but honest, kid, I felt like Devlin most had wings, his voice sounded so near all the time."

"Frost knows this place better'n we do. Gee whiz, I wish he coulda kept up with us. But he didn't, so we gotta make the best of it. I'm 'fraid to lie down in the mud, ain't you, Nickie?"

"You said it, kid! The mosquitas'll bite right through our pants. Guess we'll have to be like the birds an' roost in a tree all night, hah?"

"Yeah, I was thinkin' that too. Gee, we won't get much sleep—we *can't* sleep, 'cause maybe we'll fall out!" Skippy yawned with exhaustion. "We gotta take turns watchin' each other."

They gave up that plan after a half-hour's sentry duty on two of the lower limbs of a poplar tree. Not only were their positions uncomfortable, but the mosquitoes annoyed them despite their masks of mud. Then, too, an owl had taken up its position in a nearby tree and hooted into the awful darkness until they felt they could stand it no longer.

"Sounds like Devlin," said the superstitious Nickie. "Sounds like his spook."

"How can it be, if he ain't dead?" Skippy whispered back.

"Aw, ain't my aunt told me that some guys is so bad, they have infloo-ence on things 'round them? Well, I heard owls near that house like you did, an' how do you know Devlin didn't put the bead on one of 'em an' make it just like he is?"

"Pretty soon you'll be tellin' me you believe in imps an' all that stuff in fairy stories," Skippy said, with a little laugh.

"Aw, shut up!"

Skippy was silent, for the owl had taken the stage and drowned them out completely.

CHAPTER XXX

DEVIL'S BOG

Dawn finally came, and they waited anxiously for the light to filter through the trees sufficiently for them to be on their way. It was a disheartening sight that the light disclosed, for nothing but trees and swamp seemed to surround them and they could see no road or trail.

Skippy had been to the top of the tree, but it was not high enough for a lookout. "There's so many other trees higher'n this, it can't be done," he said, disappointed. "An' how we gonna climb those high trees when they can't be climbed, huh?"

Nickie shrugged his shoulders. "The next thing we gotta think of is chow."

Skippy grinned. "We got lots of mud—nothing but. Gee whiz, I'm hungry."

"It's too bad we couldn't 'a' knocked off that blamed owl, hah? We'd 'a' got some sleep maybe an' we'd 'a' had some breakfast on his fat neck."

They started off with high hopes. It was all a chance, Skippy reasoned, and they hadn't any idea what direction would be best. The thing to do, then, was to go and keep on going, trusting to luck that they would come out somewhere.

They wallowed through miles and miles of mud, trying with long sticks each dubious looking stretch of swamp in their path. Often they were forced to turn back and circle great pools of silent black water where on the thick green scum the thin rays of sunlight smiled in derision.

And then noonday arrived, with the sun hot and mocking directly over the tops of the trees. Below in Devil's Bog was a steaming heat that seemed to hiss out of the black, miry ground and every stir of air soon lost its freshness in the dank smell of the place.

Toward mid-afternoon Nickie lost his head a little. "S'pose we shouldn't get out, kid?" he cried. "S'pose we should go on like this for days—we'd starve—we'd be eaten up with them mosquitoes or somethin'."

Skippy tried to laugh. "I'd rather be eaten up with *somethin'*, Nickie— honest!"

"Aw, I know, kid. Here, I'm older'n you—I shouldn't lose my head. Looks like I'm yeller, hah?"

"Go on—it looks like you're mud and so'm I. Gee whiz, my aunt'd have a fit if she could see this suit. She paid six bucks for it on a Hundred and Twenty-fifth Street."

"Holy Smoke, will we ever see a Hundred and Twenty-fifth Street again! Kid, if we'd only waited a little while longer, hah? Devlin had been nosin' in that bog since he left the house an' we saw he was on his way to Hillbriar. If we'd only waited—the coast woulda been clear."

"What's the use thinkin' about 'if'? Gee whiz, we're here an' that's all there's to it. Anyway, we got each other. Poor Frost, in a way I feel kinda sorry for him if he's wand'rin' 'round like us. It must be terrible havin' no buddy to talk to in a place like this."

Nickie was touched. "I didn't think of it that way, kid. I oughta be glad an' I *am* glad. I'd know somethin' all right, all right, if I didn' have you. Didn't I say it seemed like Fate you'n me took such a shine to each other? Anyways, I felt you was regular the minute you come in the car."

Skippy looked at him. Somehow he hadn't thought about Nickie particularly—he had never defined his feelings except that he knew he disliked the boy that the old Nickie represented, the sullen, defiant and lawless Nickie. But the new Nickie, and there *was* a new one, walking and suffering beside him; he was kind, thoughtful and best of all loyal.

He put his arm through Nickie's. "I like you the way you are now—you know it! An' if you stay that way—you know what I mean—cut out the slippery stuff an' do like your aunt wants you to, I think mebbe Mr. Conne would stand your probation."

"You mean he'd get me sprung?" Nickie asked, incredulously.

"If you'd promise to be like you are now an' stick to it—that's showin' how much of a friend you are, Nickie."

Nickie stopped and put out his slim, muddy hand. "There's my mitt on it, pal!" he grinned. Then he looked puzzled. "Say, how come you got so much drag with Carlton Conne—that big dick, hah?"

It was Skippy's turn to grin. "Sump'n tells me Mr. Conne would say it was all right for me to tell *you*. Listen...."

And Nickie listened, fascinated. They trudged along arm in arm, digging into the mire before them with their sticks and forgetting, as Skippy talked, that they were weary and hungry and almost despairing.

The afternoon was waning when they noticed that the trees were beginning to thin out ahead. The underbrush was much less dense and therefore they were able to walk faster despite the fact that the ground was even more miry than any they had yet encountered.

Skippy was beginning to feel a little hope. Were they not almost out of the woods when the trees thinned out like this? He had almost convinced himself that they were, when he saw just before him several large footsteps in the slimy ground.

His finger trembled as he pointed to them. "Look, Nickie!"

Nickie nodded his head slowly and whispered, "Devlin's!"

They were standing there trying to decide whether to run or not when they saw, still a little farther on, a dark object lying on the ground. There was something so significant about its size and shape that a mutual horror of it impelled them on, despite themselves.

Frost was lying face downward in the mud.

Skippy bit at his under lip to keep from shouting. Nickie had grasped his arm and was shaking like an aspen leaf. Suddenly, they heard a sound from behind a tree not ten feet distant.

Devlin stepped out before they could move. He was grave, unsmiling as ever and his eyes glittered coldly. "Too bad, isn't it," he said enigmatically.

Skippy could only gasp; Nickie could only shake.

"It's dangerous to run off in this bog," Devlin boomed in his funereal voice. "A person can meet almost any kind of a death, as you see. You boys might be lying there instead of Frost, eh? Well, it's lucky I found you."

It was too true—Devlin had found them!

CHAPTER XXXI

DOOMED

They had neither heart nor voice to talk. Not for hours. They seemed to have lived through some terrible nightmare. From the moment when they saw Devlin's footprints the panorama had moved before them, swiftly, relentlessly. And now they were back again in the house of gloom and terror.

Skippy sat in a daze as he watched Devlin talk. "You can't complain about me as a host," he was saying, "after you deliberately desert my generous hospitality what do I do, eh? I bring you safely back and now I'm inviting you to help yourself to some supper. There's plenty of bacon and beans!"

"Aw, pipe down, Devlin!" Nickie shouted, stung into action. "What you gonna do with us, hah? That's all we wanta know!"

Devlin was calm, unruffled as ever. "I've got something to attend to," he said icily. "It can't wait. In fact, you interrupted the task by showing up when you did. But now that I have you where I know you'll be safe, I'll leave you for an hour or two. You're welcome to wash the mud from yourselves and go to bed. I can assure you that you'll be quite safe *tonight!*" He coughed significantly. "I'm leaving you boys with an easy mind—there's no Frost now to double-cross me! Goodnight!"

Skippy shivered until he was certain the man was gone. Then he got up wearily and reached for the coffee-pot. Nickie watched with some surprise.

"You got the heart to eat, hah?"

"Not the heart, Nick—just the stomach."

"Ugh! I'm sick, Skip—say, kid, ain't it great the way I just natural like call you Skippy, hah? Just like I always knew it's your name. I s'pose he's gonna put poor Frost where nobuddy'll ever find him, the same's Timmy. Ugh, I'm sick all through!"

Skippy went on with the making of the coffee, mechanically. "I can't understand 'bout the note, Nickie," he said for the hundredth time. "If Mr. Conne got it they oughta been here—gee whiz, last week. Even before."

And for the hundredth time Nickie said consolingly, "The old lady mighta lost her pocketbook in the river or sump'n, hah?" Then, after a pause: "What a break for Frost just when he was doin' us a good turn! Ain't that Fate, hah? Things just ain't right in this world."

"Listen, Nick, it's a shame about Frost an' I'm plenty thankful what he did for us—or what he tried to do. But gee whiz, he hadn't no lily-white soul to team up with Devlin, did he? He was used to rough stuff—a hold-up man, that's what he was. Well, he had a gun when he met Devlin an' he coulda made him go to the cops right that night. Gee, Frost might not been's heartless as Devlin, but he stood for Devlin's stuff. And that's as bad."

Nickie agreed. He had seemed to brighten up during Skippy's moral talk and was sniffing the air. "Holy Smoke!" he exclaimed suddenly. "Even his rotten coffee smells like food now."

Skippy smiled wanly. "Thought you wasn't hungry. Thought you was sick?"

"Guess I ain't, hah? Since I smelled that I wanta eat."

"Eat—that's right. While we live we gotta eat—gee whiz, what a life!"

"Don't talk like that, Skip. Just talk about eatin' while we can. I'll open some beans an' I'll fry some ba...."

"Oh, *not bacon!*"

"Meat'll give us strength."

"Aw, all right. But believe *me*, this is the last time in my life I'm gonna eat bacon!"

Nickie looked at him, frightened. Skippy knew what he was thinking of—he thought it himself the moment he had spoken those words. They seemed full of dreadful portent now that they had been uttered. Was it written that this was to be the last time in his life when he would eat food of any kind?

Did it mean that they were doomed?

THEY WERE FREE OF THE HOUSE SLIDING HAND OVER
HAND ALONG THE ROPE.

CHAPTER XXXII

ANOTHER DAY

They had reached a point where fear had no longer the power to torture them for sleepless hours on end. Long before Devlin returned they were sleeping the sleep of exhaustion. Fortunately, they did not hear his awesome step on the stairs nor did they hear him linger outside their door and listen to their deep, regular breathing before he went to his room for the night.

Day dawned and when the sun spread her roseate glow across the eastern horizon, Skippy got up and went on tiptoe to the window. He was amazed that he was looking out through those dirty green shutters on another day—he was amazed that Devlin had not thought of some awful fate for them before they had opened their eyes.

He looked out over the top of the rickety barn and down across forest and bog. Crickets were chirping lustily already and the sweet chorus of rising birds filled the warm air. Then a crow cawed overhead and in its wake Skippy heard sounds that pulled at his heartstrings.

A car!

He listened again. It wasn't Devlin's big car for he could see the rear of it parked in the barn. What had become of the blue coupé, he did not know. Was Frost's ghost returning in that now? He shivered and jeered at himself for absorbing Nickie's superstitions.

He seemed to sense a hushed activity going on in the clearing. His heart leaped inside his breast. He couldn't detect any particular sound—he felt impelled to go to the front room which Shorty and Biff had occupied and see if he could get a glimpse of anything or anyone through those shutters.

While he was thinking about it, he heard Devlin's heavy tread. The man came out into the hall and dashed down the stairs. Instinctively, Skippy rushed to the bed and awakened Nickie.

"I feel it, Nick!" he was whispering excitedly. "I feel it that sump'n's gonna happen an' that we better get dressed."

Nickie did not have to be told a second time—he had great regard for Skippy's hunches.

When they had dressed quickly, they ran out into the hall, but hesitated at the head of the stairs. Devlin was standing down in the front hall, evidently looking out through the small aperture in his metal door and mumbling excitedly.

"I'll not give up—*never!*" he was saying in deep, wild tones. "Neither will they get those kids—I won't give 'em the satisfaction. I'll burn the house up and they'll burn up with me, that's what I'll do! I'll show 'em—I'll show 'em!"

Skippy put his fingers to his lips and beckoned Nickie toward the rear of the hall. In a second they were scrambling up the ladder and into the attic. Then the ladder was pulled up after them and the trap door slammed shut.

Nickie was at his wit's end, crying and gesticulating. "If he lights up this dump, we'll roast fine up here. What's the idea, hah—what's the idea? That guy must be cuckoo."

"I'll take a chance on him burnin'," Skippy said, running toward the front window, "but he ain't gonna use that silencer on me!"

He paused at the window and gasped. The clearing was full of men—he couldn't seem to count them. Men in uniform, men without uniform, and in the group he saw one that he recognized instantly because of a certain jauntiness of bearing and a cigar that was being chewed with a peculiar fierceness from one side to the other in the man's generous mouth.

"*Mr. Conne—Mr. Conne!*" Skippy cried, wild with delight. "It's *me*—up here. Me and Nickie—Nickie Fallon!"

Carlton Conne pushed his derby hat almost off his head and as he looked up his cigar went to the side of his mouth and remained there at a right angle.

"Kid!" he shouted. "You there, eh? You all right?"

"Yeah!" Skippy was gasping. "But we can't...." He took hold of the bars one at a time and shook them ferociously, with Nickie's help, of course, to prove what he was saying, "We can't get out through these ... these...."

Nickie shrieked! Something had happened. "The bars, kid! Look, *they're loose!*"

Skippy looked in amazement. Miracles didn't happen of course. He remembered that they had had to leave their task quite hurriedly the last time they had been up there—it might have happened that they had worked the bars loose enough to wrench away, but in their haste had not discovered it.

Nickie was straining himself to the very utmost until he had worked them away sufficiently for them to get their bodies through the window.

Skippy was feverishly engaged in swinging his lariat over to the evergreen tree to the accompaniment of joyous shouts.

And then they were free of the house, sliding hand over hand along the taut rope until they reached the sturdy tree. Fallon got safely to the ground first, and as Skippy followed he noticed great curls of thick smoke pouring out from the shutters on the lower floor.

Somebody shouted, "We'll get in at him the same way the kids came out, hey, Conne—through the attic?"

"Don't bother!" Mr. Conne was saying in his brusque manner. "We'll take no chances on losing any lives. Let Dean Devlin roast. He deserves it now—and hereafter too."

Skippy was delighted that he was having his hand shaken by the greatest detective in his country. It was the longest handshake he had ever experienced. And, what was more wonderful still, Carlton Conne's arm was about his shoulder.

"We only got your note last night, kid," he was saying. "Your sweet old lady didn't get out her pocketbook until yesterday afternoon when she wanted to go out for a walk, after being laid up with a cold. She took the train and came straight to New York."

"I'm sorry, Mr. Conne—I'm sorry...."

"What are you sorry for? You've been a clever youngster through this whole thing—that note was a masterpiece."

"I wrote it like that in case Devlin should find it on me, then he wouldn't know I was sort of workin' for you," Skippy said apologetically.

"Couldn't have done better myself!" Mr. Conne said crisply.

"We doped out the distance from the way you figured the time and your idea of telling how the house came to be left here and about the hermit. We knew you were somewhere in this section because Dick Hallam reported he spotted you in Hillbriar. I learned only yesterday from an insurance company complaint that an apparent systematic effort was being made to defraud by insuring boys and doing away with them to collect on the policies. I got Hallam on the phone, had him check in Hillbriar and he dug up the evidence that linked Devlin unmistakably to the racket. And a few hours later, just before I got your note, I received the information that Devlin, who had been in an insane asylum, when we thought he was under cover and had escaped, had developed a mania for killing while being apparently normal in other respects."

He patted Skippy on the back and then went on: "So I prayed for a break that we might get to you in time. I blamed myself for putting you in such danger, but I never knew Devlin as a killer and I never suspected the racket he was working, or I wouldn't have sent you on the job. Well, thank God we made it in time."

"It's all right, it's all right, Boss," Skippy answered.

"Yeah, it is—now," Nickie agreed.

Mr. Conne put the boys in his car and got in beside them. "We'll wait and see this thing go up in smoke, eh? I always thought I didn't have anything cruel in me, but darned if I don't enjoy knowing that that smoke is taking Dean Devlin with it. It's almost too good for him—he should suffer for making kids suffer."

"Yeah, poor Timmy," Skippy sighed.

"Yes, I've got in touch with his aunt in Glens Falls. We traced him when you wrote his name was Timmy Brogan. You haven't any idea where Devlin put him?"

"No, an' we don't know where he put Frost last night," Skippy said, telling that part of their tragic story. "I feel sorry about him too, Mr. Conne, but it's Timmy we'll never forget. He mighta got away if he hadn't come back from the creek to warn us about Devlin. He was like a hero, Timmy was."

Mr. Conne thought so too, but was too much absorbed to say very much. "I'm glad Fallon escaped with you, kid," he said, smiling at Nickie. "Your aunt's been worrying the police department day and night to find out where you were."

"Yeah?" Nickie said abashed. "Holy smoke, I'll be glad seein' her again."

Skippy grinned. "Nickie an' me—gee whiz, we'd gone crazy if we hadn't been able to talk to each other. That house...."

"Never mind, kid," Mr. Conne said soothingly. "It's all over now, and I guess you're good and sick of this business, eh? It's a rotten game and your Aunt Min says she'll never let you out of her sight...."

"Say, listen, Mr. Conne," Skippy interposed excitedly, "I can talk Aunt Min into lettin' me do anything—I ain't worryin' about her. It's you—will you gimme that job you promised me? If you say I did good...."

Mr. Conne tilted his cigar up in the corner of his mouth and looked at Skippy quizzically. "Now I might consider that job, kid," he said, half smiling, "if you'll promise to keep that smudge off your face when you come into my office. I notice it's dirty—and so early in the morning!"

"Aw, that's mud from yesterday—we put it on for the mosquitoes! Anyway, will you do one thing more, huh, Mr. Conne?"

"What?"

"Nickie's promised to be awful good so will you go his probation 'cause any judge would do that for a feller if *you* went his probation—gee whiz!"

"I think the answer to that will be *yes*, kid. But suppose we get away from here now, eh? It's getting a little too hot even for me. I haven't had my breakfast and I suppose you kids haven't either. We'll stop at a nice lunch-wagon I noticed down on the highway and we'll have fried eggs and...."

"Gee whiz, Mr. Conne!" Skippy interrupted. "If you're gonna say we'll have bacon, please don't say it!"

"No? Why not?" Carlton Conne had started the car and was waiting, expectantly. "I thought all kids loved bacon."

"Sure, we did," Skippy answered. "Nickie an' me loved it like you say, but not now. Let's go an' eat, huh?"

"Yeah," Nickie said eagerly, "let's scram. Sometime we'll tell about that bacon, Mr. Conne." Skippy nodded, took a long, last look at the burning house and turned to Mr. Conne. "It's a sad story."

"What is?" the detective asked.

"The bacon," Skippy answered simply.

THE END

9 789362 517388